P9-CSC-520

Chinglish

BOOKS BY DAVID HENRY HWANG
AVAILABLE FROM TCG

Chinglish

Flower Drum Song
Book by David Henry Hwang
Music by Richard Rodgers
Lyrics by Oscar Hammerstein II

Golden Child

Trying to Find Chinatown
INCLUDES:

Bondage
The Dance and the Railroad
Family Devotions
FOB
The House of Sleeping Beauties
The Sound of a Voice
Trying to Find Chinatown
The Voyage

Yellow Face

Chinglish

A PLAY

David Henry Hwang

Chinese translations
by Candace Mui Ngam Chong

Chinese language editing
by Joanna C. Lee

THEATRE COMMUNICATIONS GROUP
NEW YORK
2012

Chinglish is copyright © 2012 by David Henry Hwang

Chinglish is published by Theatre Communications Group, Inc.,
520 Eighth Avenue, 24th Floor, New York, NY 10018-4156

All Rights Reserved. Except for brief passages quoted in newspaper, magazine, radio or television reviews, no part of this book may be reproduced in any form or by any means, electronic or mechanical, including photocopying or recording, or by an information storage and retrieval system, without permission in writing from the publisher.

Professionals and amateurs are hereby warned that this material, being fully protected under the Copyright Laws of the United States of America and all other countries of the Berne and Universal Copyright Conventions, is subject to a royalty. All rights, including but not limited to, professional, amateur, recording, motion picture, recitation, lecturing, public reading, radio and television broadcasting, and the rights of translation into foreign languages are expressly reserved. Particular emphasis is placed on the question of readings and all uses of this book by educational institutions, permission for which must be secured from the author's representative: William Craver, Paradigm, 360 Park Avenue South, 16th Floor, New York, NY 10010, (212) 897-6400.

The publication of *Chinglish* by David Henry Hwang through TCG's Book Program is made possible in part by the New York State Council on the Arts with the support of Governor Andrew Cuomo and the New York State Legislature.

TCG books are exclusively distributed to the book trade by Consortium Book Sales and Distribution.

CIP data information is on file at the Library of Congress, Washington, D.C.

ISBN: 978-1-55936-410-2

Book design and composition by Lisa Govan
First Edition, May 2012

Chinglish

Chinglish was developed at the Lark Play Development Center (John Eisner, Artistic Director; Michael Robertson, Managing Director), New York City, in association with The Public Theater (Oskar Eustis, Artistic Director), New York City.

Chinglish premiered at the Goodman Theatre (Robert Falls, Artistic Director; Roche Schulfer, Executive Director) on June 18, 2011. It was directed by Leigh Silverman; the set design was by David Korins, the costume design was by Anita Yavich, the lighting design was by Brian MacDevitt, the projection design was by Jeff Sugg and Shawn Duan, the sound design was by Darron L. West; the cultural advisors were Joanna C. Lee and Ken Smith, the Mandarin Chinese translator was Candace Mui Ngam Chong, the production stage manager was Alden Vasquez and the dramaturgs were Oskar Eustis and Tanya Palmer. The cast was:

DANIEL CAVANAUGH	James Waterston
PETER TIMMS	Stephen Pucci
CAI GUOLIANG	Larry Lei Zhang
XI YAN	Jennifer Lim
QIAN/PROSECUTOR LI	Angela Lin
BING/JUDGE GEMING	Johnny Wu
ZHAO	Christine Lin
UNDERSTUDIES	Norm Boucher, Angela Lin, Brian Nishii, Clara Wong

Chinglish was produced on Broadway by Jeffrey Richards, Jerry Frankel, Jay and Cindy Gutterman/Cathy Chernoff, Heni Koenigsberg/Lily Fan, Joseph and Matthew Deitch, Dasha Epstein, Ronald and Marc Frankel, Barry and Carole Kaye, Mary Lu Roffe, The Broadway Consortium, Ken Davenport, Filerman Bensinger, Herbert Goldsmith, Jam Theatricals, Olympus Theatricals, Playful Productions, David and Barbara Stoller, Roy Gottlieb and Hunter Arnold, in association with the Goodman Theatre, and Jeremy Scott Blaustein, associate producer. It opened at the Longacre Theatre on October 27, 2011, with these changes: Daniel Cavanaugh was played by Gary Wilmes; the understudies were Tony Carlin, Angela Lin, Brian Nishii and Vivian Chiu; the production stage manager was Stephen M. Kaus.

CHARACTERS

DANIEL CAVANAUGH: a businessman, Caucasian, American, forties

PETER TIMMS: a consultant, Caucasian, British, forties

CAI GUOLIANG: the Cultural Minister, Chinese, male, fifties

XI YAN: Vice Minister of Culture, Chinese, female, forties

MISS QIAN: a translator, Chinese

BING: Cai's nephew, a translator, Chinese, twenties

ZHAO: a translator, Chinese, female

JUDGE XU GEMING: Xi's husband, forty to fifty (played by the actor who plays Bing)

PROSECUTOR LI: female, thirties (played by the actor who plays Qian)

WAITER, HOTEL MANAGER, DRIVER: doubling at director's discretion

NOTE

Cast breakdown: 2 Caucasian males, 3 Asian females, 2 Asian males.

SETTING

The present. An American assembly room and the city of Guiyang, China.

EDITOR'S NOTE ON LANGUAGE

Dialogue is spoken in Mandarin Chinese, the modern standard language known in China as Putonghua (or "common language"). Dialogue in bold indicates English translation (displayed in supertitles in production) of dialogue spoken in modern standard Chinese. Note: the English translation doesn't always match the Mandarin.

Chinese dialogue will be displayed in two formats: traditional characters: 繁體中文 and pinyin, the Romanization system from the People's Republic of China.

For instructional purposes today, most people in America, Australia and Europe learn Putonghua using the pinyin system, which has four standardized tones for vowel pronunciation, numerically arranged: 1st tone (high, marked ā, ē, ī, ō, ū); 2nd tone (high rising, marked á, é, í, ó, ú), 3rd tone (low falling-rising, marked ǎ, ě, ǐ, ǒ, ǔ), 4th tone (high falling, marked à, è, ì, ò, ù) and also the neutral tone, which is not marked.

As with any complex tonal language, there are exceptions to pronunciation rules. These are often adjustments to facilitate the flow of the language. One such example is the word "bù" (不), which is the negating adverb, usually pronounced in the 4th tone. However, when it is used before another 4th tone, it changes to the 2nd tone (bú). Another exception is the succession of words in the 3rd tone, when all will change to the 2nd tone except the final 3rd tone. Chinese characters sometimes have multiple pronunciations (changing in tones, sometimes even changing the vowels), depending on context, and whether they are used as verbs or nouns.

While normally "tonal changes" are not marked in standard printed pinyin, we have made all of the adjustments as a guide to reading the words aloud. For ease in referencing Chinese characters to their romanizations, we have kept each Chinese word separate and distinct, rather than forming composite nouns and verbs per standard pinyin practice.

Dialogue intended to be communicated through gesture rather than verbally will be indicated by carrot brackets (< >).

A double-dash (//) indicates when the next speech begins, overlapping the preceding dialogue.

—Ken Smith

Act One

———

Scene 1

Daniel Cavanaugh, a white American, forties, speaks to us at a podium, wireless clicker in hand. Images from his presentation appear upstage.

First image: a photograph of a sign, in both English and Chinese. The Chinese reads: 注意安全坡道路滑 *。The English reads:* ***"To Take Notice of Safe: The Slippery Are Very Crafty."***

DANIEL: "To take notice of safe: The slippery are very crafty." The proper translation should be: "Slippery Slopes Ahead."

(Click: second image. The Chinese reads: 财务处处长 *。The English reads:* ***"Financial Affairs Is Everywhere Long."***)

What does this one mean? Believe it or not: "Chief Financial Officer." Likely the result of a bad computer translation program.

(Click: third image. The Chinese reads: 干货计价处 *。The English reads:* ***"Fuck the Certain Price of Goods."***)

Surprisingly, this sign does not have anything to do with a sale. Who wouldn't be thrilled to walk into, say, Barneys and find a sign reading: "Fuck the Certain Price of Goods"? But it should actually read: "Dry Goods Pricing Department." Unfortunately.

(Pause.)

You see, after the Communist government came to power, Chairman Mao ordered that the centuries-old system of writing Chinese characters—beautiful, arcane, devilishly complicated—be simplified for the "masses"—or, as we would call them today, "consumers." In so doing, the ideographs for "dry" and "to do" were merged. And "to do" is also slang for, well, to "do" someone. Once you know that, it all makes sense.

(Pause.)

Thank you to the Commerce League of Ohio for inviting me to talk about doing business in China. The greatest pool of untapped consumers history has ever known. People ask me, How did I manage to get a foothold there? Well, the truth is, when I started out, I knew nothing more about China than the difference between Moo Shu Pork and General Tso's Chicken.

(Pause.)

The first rule of doing business in China is also the last. Assuming you are an American. Because, if you are American, it is also safe to assume that you do not speak a single fucking foreign language. If you take away nothing else from our talk today, remember this. Write it down.

(Pause.)

When doing business in China, always bring your own translator.

Scene 2

A title reads: "Three Years Earlier. Guiyang, China." Daniel sits with Peter Timms, a white Englishman, forties, in a restaurant in the provincial capital of Guiyang.

DANIEL: I run a small, family-owned firm, based in Cleveland. Have you seen our website?

PETER: Impressive.

DANIEL: I sent you our proposal. My // assistant—

PETER: It's a fine proposal.

DANIEL: Thank you. So, can we make something happen here?

PETER: I can arrange a meeting with Cai Guoliang, Minister of Culture for Guiyang City.

DANIEL: Great.

PETER: But I need to make sure you're prepared. I suppose you've heard of "Guanxi."

DANIEL: Bring me up to speed.

PETER: Relationships. It's almost a cliché now, but business in China is built on relationships.

DANIEL: This is the part about taking them out. Wining and dining.

PETER: Wining and dining are just the beginning. You see, for years, Western economists have held that a fair and consistent legal system—with predictable outcomes—is necessary for solid economic growth.

DANIEL: You have to know the rules of the game.

PETER: Precisely. But, here in China, the legal system is a joke. No one expects justice. And yet, the Chinese have maintained consistent growth over decades, at levels the West can only dream about.

DANIEL: With no justice system.

PETER: But what you *do* have, are predictable outcomes.

DANIEL: Mmmm.

PETER: People here know roughly what to expect. The trick is to understand that all these outcomes take place *outside* the formal justice system.

DANIEL: Through—

PETER: Guanxi.

DANIEL: Guanxi.

PETER: Which means, you have to take the time and trouble to build an actual relationship.

DANIEL: OK.

PETER: Otherwise, you leave here with merely a signed contract?

DANIEL: Contracts mean nothing here.

PETER: Because—

DANIEL: Contracts are shit?

PETER: Because the legal system—

DANIEL: —means nothing here.

PETER: Precisely. The only thing that matters is—

DANIEL: —the relationship.

PETER: Guanxi.

DANIEL: Guanxi. I got it.

(Pause.)

So I should think about staying here more than a week.

PETER: Try eight, Mr. Cavanaugh.

DANIEL: Daniel. Eight weeks?

PETER: For a first visit, Daniel.

DANIEL: My family is gonna kill me.

(Pause.)

What am I eating?

PETER: Sour fish soup.

DANIEL: Spicy.

PETER: The Guizhou people pride themselves on their peppers.

DANIEL: Can I get a cold soda or something?

PETER *(To offstage)*: Lái gè bīng zhèn ké kóu kě lè, bú yào jiā bīng.
來個冰鎮可口可樂, 不要加冰 。
One cold Coca-Cola, no ice.

DANIEL: How do I get this? —You speak Chinese.

PETER: Passably.

DANIEL: Well, of course, you speak—

PETER: No, actually, very well.

DANIEL: You've been here in China for—

PETER: Nineteen years. I always forget, when I'm talking to a Westerner, to boast about myself.

DANIEL: And when you're with Chinese people, you have to be all—

PETER: Criticize yourself. But make sure there's someone else in the room who will contradict you—ideally, at great length.

(A Waiter brings a soft drink. Daniel drinks.)

When I first arrived in China, to teach English at Nanjing University, a woman told me, "Your students are going to expect you to be a rich and successful Westerner. Play up to their image—the Chinese love big gamblers—win or lose, it doesn't even matter, they want to see you as a high-roller. Then, they'll respect you."

DANIEL: A high-roller.

PETER: So, when I first met the student body, I reeled off my achievements, made myself sound very grand. Afterwards, my sponsor took me aside and explained, "Anyone who's really great, doesn't need to say so." And that made sense to me. So I started reading Chinese philosophy, studying calligraphy, porcelains, folk dancing. And founded my consultancy firm.

DANIEL: So at these meetings, if I'm all humble, you'll be there to contradict me?

PETER: Should you choose to engage my services.

DANIEL: You work on commission, right?

PETER: I can. // I feel—

DANIEL: Your website suggested // some flexibility in—

PETER: I appreciate that yours is a completely // speculative venture.

DANIEL: I'm taking a chance // on you, too.

PETER: Right. // My usual—

DANIEL: So we can dispense with any upfront retainer fee.

PETER: I'm open to that kind of arrangement.

DANIEL: I have a board—

PETER: My usual commission—

DANIEL: My brother and the others would // have to approve—

PETER: My usual commission is fifteen percent of your deal.

DANIEL: Fifteen percent.

PETER: Right.

DANIEL: Isn't it normally ten?

PETER: Yes, well—

DANIEL: I think I can get my board to support ten.

PETER: But without an upfront retainer fee, my backend needs to go // a bit—

DANIEL: All right. Twelve.

PETER: Really? Yes. Twelve.

DANIEL: I'll tell them, you've been helping businesses here for— your website // said—

PETER: Almost a decade.

DANIEL: Impressive. And if my brother complains—he doesn't have a clue what's going on over here, does he?

PETER: With all due respect, no, he doesn't.

DANIEL: Eight weeks. OK, let's throw the dice. Be one of those high-rollers.

PETER: We have a deal?

DANIEL: I want you to get me some Guanxi.

Scene 3

Office of the Minister, Cai, fifties. He wears a suit and smokes. Also present are Vice Minister Xi Yan, female, forties, also wearing Western clothes, along with Qian, a female translator, and Daniel and Peter.

DANIEL: We're a small family firm.

QIAN: Tā nà jiā shì xiǎo gōng sī, méi shén me míng qì de.
他 那 家 是 小 公司, 沒什麼 名氣 的 。
His company is tiny and insignificant.

DANIEL: Started by my great-grandfather in 1925.

QIAN: Gōng sī shì tā zǔ xiān zài èr shí shì jì chū jiàn lì de.
公司 是 他 祖先 在 二十世紀 初 建立 的 。
His ancestor founded it in the early twentieth century.

PETER: É hài é zhōu zhāo pái shè jì gōng sī shì qí zhōng yī jiā zhòng
yào de zhāo pái zhì zào gōng chǎng
俄亥俄州 招牌 設計 公司 是 其中一家 重要 的 招牌 製造
工廠,
Ohio Signage is one of the major manufacturers

shì měi guó zhōng xī bù zuì jù sù zhì de zhāo pái zhì zào gōng chǎng,
是 美國 中 西部 最 具 素質 的 招牌 製造 工廠,
of top-quality signage in the American Midwest,

fú wù dì qū bāo kuò zhī jiā gē.
服務 地區 包括 芝加哥 。
the region which includes Chicago.

CAI: Ah! Chicago!
DANIEL: Chicago? No, we're based in—
PETER *(To Daniel)*: Your firm is based in Cleveland, but you've done
business in—
DANIEL: Chicago.
CAI: Chicago.

QIAN: Zhī jiā gē yǒu tā chù lì de zhāo pái,
芝加哥 有 他 矗立 的 招牌,
He has erected signs in Chicago,

dàn tā gè rén lái zì bú zhù míng de xiǎo cūn zhuāng.
但 他 個人 來自 不著 名 的 小 村莊 。
but his home village is insignificant.

CAI: Wó lǎo jiā yě shì gè xiǎo cūn zhuāng.
我 老家 也 是 個 小 村莊 。
I also come from a small village.

QIAN *(To Daniel)*: Minister Cai was also—
PETER *(To Daniel)*: The Minister says—

(Pause. To Qian:)

Ō, bù hǎo yì si.
噢, 不好意思 。
Oh, excuse me.

QIAN *(To Peter)*: Bào qiàn.
抱歉 。
Forgive me.

(To Daniel) Minister Cai was also born in a small farming village.
DANIEL: Cleveland isn't exactly a farming—though I suppose it was at one time.

QIAN *(To Cai)*: Tā shuō nà bian de tǔ dì zǎo jiù huāng wú le.
他 說 那邊 的 土地 早就 荒蕪 了。
He says their crops failed long ago.

XI *(Exasperated)*: Kè lǐ fū lán!
克 里 夫 蘭 !
Cleveland!

Kǎ fán nuò xiān sheng shì lái zì kè lǐ fū lán!
卡凡諾 先生 是 來自 克 里 夫 蘭 !
Mr. Cavanaugh is from Cleveland!

Bú shì dà chéng shì, dàn yě shì yí gè zhòng yào de zhì zào zhōng xīn.
不是 大城市, 但 也 是 一個 重要 的 製造 中心 。
Not a major city, but a significant manufacturing center.

PETER: Xiè xie fù jú zhǎng.

謝謝副局長 。

Thank you, Vice Minister.

XI: Huò zhě shuō céng jīng zhòng yào guò, zài měi guó hái yǒu zhì
zào yè de nián dài.

或者 說 曾經 重要 過, 在 美國 還有 製造 業 的 年代 。

Or it was, back when the U.S. still manufactured things.

DANIEL: We used to be a factory town, but // nowadays—

PETER *(To Daniel)*: We've sorted all that out.

DANIEL: Oh. Anyway, Ohio Signage has managed to acquire a repu-
tation for quality work. Have you seen our website?

PETER: Nǐ kàn guò tā men de wǎng zhàn ma?

你 看 過 他們 的 網站 嗎 ？

Have you seen their website?

CAI: Hěn bú cuò.

很不 錯 。

Impressive.

PETER *(To Daniel)*: He likes your website.

(To Cai:)

Tā de jiā zú bǎ é hài é zhōu zhāo pái shè jì gōng sī,

他 的 家族 把 俄亥俄州 招牌 設計 公司,

His family has built Ohio Signage,

dǎ zào chéng měi guó zuì zhuó yuè de qǐ yè zhī yī.

打 造成 美國 最 卓越 的 企業 之一 。

into one of America's most illustrious businesses.

CAI: Zhī jiā gē! wǒ qù guò zhī jiā gē!

芝加哥 ！我 去 過 芝加哥 ！

Chicago! I have visited Chicago!

(Pause; to Qian:)

Gào su tā yā!
告訴 他 呀！
Tell him!

QIAN *(To Daniel)*: The Minister has visited Chicago.
DANIEL *(To Peter)*: We're back to—?

(To Cai:)

We work there all the time.
PETER: Zhī jiā gē dào chù dōu shì kǎ fán nuò xiān sheng zhì zào de
zhāo pái.
芝加哥 到處 都 是 卡凡諾 先生 製造 的 招牌。
Mr. Cavanaugh's signs hang all over Chicago.

CAI: Nà shì gè wěi dà de chéng shì.
那 是 個 偉大 的 城市。
It is a great city.

QIAN: The Minister enjoys this city very much.
DANIEL: Who doesn't like Chicago?

QIAN: Tā rèn tóng nín de shuō fǎ.
他 認同 您 的 說法。
He agrees.

DANIEL *(To Cai)*: You'll have to let me show you around sometime.

QIAN: Xià cì yóu tā zuò dōng.
下 次 由 他 作東。
He will be your host there.

CAI: Wǒ zài zhī jiā gē de shí hòu zuì xǐ huān chī niú pái.
我 在 芝加哥 的時候 最 喜歡 吃 牛排。
When I'm in Chicago, I like to eat steak.

QIAN: He enjoys to consume your American beef-cows.

DANIEL: My—? Ah! Smith & Wollensky?

(Pause. Qian looks at Daniel. Daniel looks at Peter.)

(To Peter) Smith & Wollensky?

(Off Peter's confusion:)

A steakhouse. You've never—? The place is like my second home!

PETER: Oh!

QIAN: I see!
Tā shì shuō—
他 是 說—
He's referring to—

PETER: Smith & Wollensky.

QIAN: yī jiā niú pái diàn, tā yǒu shí hòu zhù zài nà lǐ.
一家 牛排 店, 他 有時候 住 在 那裡 。
a steak restaurant, where he sometimes lives.

PETER: Bù! tā bú zhù zài nà lǐ—
不 ! 他 不住 在 那裡—
No, he doesn't—

(To Cai:)

Nà shì zhī jiā gē zuì hǎo de niú pái diàn, tā xiáng qǐng nín qù
cháng cháng.
那 是 芝加哥 最好 的 牛排 店, 他 想 請 您 去 嚐嚐 。
It's the best in Chicago, and he wants to invite you.

CAI: Xiè xie!
謝謝 !
Thank you!

QIAN *(To Peter)*: Duì bu qǐ.

對不起。

Forgive me.

PETER: Bú yào jǐn—

不要緊—

No need to—

QIAN: Wǒ de yīng yǔ bù hǎo.

我的 英語 不好。

My English is so poor.

PETER: Bù! hén hǎo!

不！很好！

It's excellent!

QIAN: Ér nǐ de zhōng wén—

而 你 的 中文—

But your Chinese—

PETER: Nà lǐ, nà lǐ . . .

那裡、那裡……

No, no, no . . .

CAI *(To Peter)*: Tā shuō de duì, nǐ de pǔ tōng huà shuō de bǐ wǒ ér zi
hái yào hǎo!

她說得對, 你的普通話說得比我兒子還要好！

She's right, your Chinese is better than my own child's!

PETER: Jú zhǎng tài kuā jiǎng le.

局長 太 誇獎 了。

The Minister is too kind.

CAI *(Referring to Peter)*:

Wǒ jiù shuō, zhè lǎo wài shì gè háo lǎo shī.

我 就 說, 這 老外 是 個 好 老師。

That's why this foreigner is such a good teacher.

Dì yī cì jiàn miàn wǒ jiù xiǎng,

第一次 見面 我 就 想,

The first time I met him, I thought,

tā néng jiào góu yě xué huì shuō yīng wén!

他 能 叫 狗 也 學會 說 英文！

He could teach English to a dog!

PETER: Xiè xie, xiè xie.

謝謝, 謝謝 。

Thank you, thank you.

(They all laugh. Daniel tries to laugh along.
  To Daniel:)

They're talking about my Chinese.

DANIEL: Which is amazing, right?

QIAN *(To Cai)*: Jiù lián wú zhī de lǎo wài dōu míng bái!

就 連 無知 的 老外 都 明白！

Even the illiterate foreigner knows!

CAI *(To Daniel, referring to Peter)*: Tā zhōng guó huà shuō dé hǎo jí le.

他 中國話 說 得 好 極了 。

His Chinese is excellent.

QIAN: Not like my English.

XI: Bǐ dé zhōng guó huà de chéng dù, wǒ men dōu dá chéng gòng shí le!

彼得 中國話 的 程度, 我們 都 達成 共識 了！

All right, we all agree about Peter's Chinese!

Xiàn zài ké yǐ jì xù tán jì huà shū le ma?

現在 可以 繼續 談 計劃書 了 嗎 ？

Can we move on to the proposal?

QIAN *(To Daniel)*: Vice Minister Xi agrees on the quality of Peter's Chinese. And also wishes to discuss your proposal.

DANIEL: Great. Well—

CAI: Hěn bú cuò.

很不錯 。

It's very impressive.

Suī rán jià gé—xiāng duì běn dì de biāo zhǔn lái shuō, bǐ jiào guì.

雖然價格—相對本地的標準來說, 比較貴 。

Though the price—rather high, by local standards.

QIAN: He likes your proposal, but—so expensive!

DANIEL: I understand. That's why I appreciate this chance to—

CAI: Jìn guǎn rú cǐ, wǒ hái shì yuàn yì

儘管如此, 我還是願意

Nevertheless, I would like to give

rèn zhēn dì kǎo lǜ pìn yòng nǐ de gōng sī.

認真地考慮聘用你的公司 。

serious consideration to hiring your firm.

QIAN: Despite so expensive, he will still consider your proposal.

DANIEL: Thank you. And here's why we're worth the money.

QIAN: Tā huì jiě shì wèi shén me tā huā qián huì nà me dà shǒu dà jiǎo.

他會解釋為什麼他花錢會那麼大手大腳 。

He will explain why he spends money so recklessly.

PETER: Shì xiǎng shuō míng tā de zhuān cháng jiāng rú hé bāng zhù guì yáng.

是想說明他的專長將如何幫助貴陽 。

Why his expertise can help Guiyang.

QIAN *(To Cai, referring to Peter)*: Duì, xiàng tā suǒ shuō de.

對, 像他所說的。

Yes, like he says.

PETER *(To Qian)*: Bào qiàn, yào shì wǒ—

抱歉, 要是我—

Forgive me if I—

QIAN: Bù, bú yào jǐn—wǒ biān tīng biān xué.

不, 不要緊—我邊聽邊學。

No, no—I will listen and learn.

(Pause. Daniel looks to Peter for a cue to begin. Peter nods.)

DANIEL: Minister Cai, you are building a world-class Arts Center.

PETER: Quán shì jiè dōu zhī dào guì yáng de jīng jì jiāng yào téng fēi,

全世界都知道貴陽的經濟將要騰飛,

The whole world knows of the economic prosperity coming to Guiyang,

tā men dōu zài qī dài nǐ men nà suǒ shì jiè jí yì shù zhōng xīn de kāi mù.

他們都在期待你們那所世界級藝術中心的開幕。

and awaits the opening of your world-class Arts Center.

(His rhythm is thrown by Peter's translation; Daniel continues:)

DANIEL: OK. You've brought in a German architect, you'll be using Brazilian wood, Italian marble, a state-of-the-art sound system designed by Japanese engineers. But what about the signs? Are they going to match up to—?

PETER: Nǐ men yǐn jìn de dé guó jiàn zhù shī, bā xī mù cái,

你們引進的德國建築師 、巴西木材 、

You've brought in a German architect, Brazilian wood,

yì dà lì dà lǐ shí, rì běn yīn xiǎng, zhè xiē quán dōu shì dì yī liú de.

意大利大理石 、日本音響, 這些全都是第一流的 。

Italian marble, Japanese sound engineers, all first-rate.

DANIEL: Yes, and anyway—but the signs, are they going to live up to the same high standards? Take, for example—

PETER: Kě duì yú guǎn nèi de zhǐ shì pái,
可對於館內的指示牌,
But where it comes to the signs,

wǒ men yīng gāi jí qǔ qí tā shěng shì zhèng fǔ de jiào xùn.
我們應該汲取其他省市政府的教訓 。
we must learn from the mistakes of other municipalities.

Pì rú shuō—
譬如說—
For example—

(Cai's cell phone goes off. He answers it.)

CAI: Wèi?
喂 ?
Hello?

Rén mín jiě fàng jūn zěn me la?
人民解放軍怎麼啦 ?
The People's Liberation Army?

Tā mén de zhàn dòu lì què shí hěn qiáng,
他們的戰鬥力確實很強,
They might be good at fighting,

kě shōu dào gǎo yīn yuè jù wán quán bù xíng.
可說到搞音樂劇完全不行 。
but they're lousy at producing musicals.

Bù!

不！

No!

(Cai hangs up, looks expectantly at Daniel.)

PETER *(To Daniel)*: <Go on.>

DANIEL: Right. So we were . . . talking about these other cities. For instance, Shanghai.

PETER: Pì rú shuō shàng hǎi.

譬如說上海。

Consider Shanghai.

DANIEL: The Pudong Grand Theatre.

PETER: Pǔ dōng dà jù yuàn.

浦東大劇院。

The Pudong Grand Theatre.

DANIEL: At the opening—the foreign business people and officials— did they notice the woods or the fixtures? No, they were all laughing!

PETER: Kāi mù nà tiān, nà xiē wài guó rén dōu zài xiào.

開幕那天, 那些外國人都在笑。

At the opening, the foreigners—were laughing.

(Daniel and Peter finally begin to find a rhythm.)

DANIEL: At the signs—because the translations were so bad!

PETER: Yīn wèi zhǐ shì pái shàng de fān yì—

因為指示牌上的翻譯—

At the signs—because the translations were—

shí zài bù wán měi!
實在不完美 ！
imperfect!

DANIEL: Restrooms for the handicapped—good thing, right?

PETER: Jǔ yī gè lì zi, shāng cán rén shì xí shǒu jiān?
舉一個例子, 傷殘人士洗手間—
For example, the handicapped restrooms?

DANIEL: Not when the sign reads, "Deformed Man's Toilet."

(To Peter:)

Can you translate that?
PETER: Never fear.

Fān chéng「jī xíng nán rén de cè suǒ」.
翻成「 畸形男人的廁所 」。
Read, "Deformed Man's Toilet."

CAI: Wǒ men tīng shuō guo, tài diū rén le.
我們聽說過, 太丟人了 。
We heard about that, terrible.

QIAN: The Minister knows of this disgrace. And he is embarrassed.
DANIEL: And in the ladies' room: "Wash After Relief."

PETER: Zài nǚ cè nèi de「rú cè hòu chōng shuǐ」.
在女廁內的「如廁後沖水 」。
And the ladies' washroom: "Wash After Relief."

DANIEL: "Slip and Fall Down Carefully."
PETER: That's good—you can . . .
DANIEL: I could go on, but my point is—

PETER: Tā de zhòng diǎn shì—
他的重點是—
His point is—

DANIEL: Who cares about the money they spent on all the other stuff? If I went there, what I would remember is the sign that said: "Don't Forget to Carry Your Thing."

PETER: Tā zhǐ huì jì dé zhǐ shì pái xiě zhe 「bié wàng jì dài zóu nǐ de lǎo èr」.
他只會記得指示牌寫著「別忘記帶走你的老二」。
He would remember the sign reading: "Don't Forget to Carry Your Thing."

CAI: Gòu le.
夠了。
That's enough.

DANIEL: Minister Cai, the money you spend now is a small price to avoid big embarrassment later.

PETER: Tā zhōng xīn jiàn yì nín jīn tiān xiān huā yī diǎn qián
他衷心建議您今天先花一點錢
He respectfully suggests that spending a little money now

yǐ bì miǎn jiāng lái miàn zi shàng gèng dà de sǔn shī.
以避免將來面子上更大的損失。
will save Guiyang great loss of face later.

CAI: Nǐ men tí chū de wèn tí hěn zhòng yào,
你們提出的問題很重要,
You raise some very salient points,

jiù shì zuò wéi yī gè zhēn zhèng de guó jì wén huà zhōng xīn,
就是作為一個真正的國際文化中心,
about the importance of the signs,

qí zhǐ shì pái de zhòng yào xìng.
其指示牌的重要性 。
in a truly international Cultural Center.

(Cai shoots a look at Qian.)

Xiǎo qián.
小錢 。
Miss Qian.

QIAN *(Who had let her mind drift)*: Oh! Um—the Minister, he—wants to create an international Cultural Center. Truly.

CAI: Wǒ xī wàng guì yáng néng zhǎn xiàn zhōng guó de chuán tǒng yì shù.
我希望貴陽能展現中國的傳統藝術 。
I want Guiyang to showcase the traditional Chinese arts.

QIAN: The Minister enjoys the art which is old and unpopular.

CAI: Pì rú shuō wǒ men de jīng jù tuán.
譬如說我們的京劇團 。
Such as our local Beijing Opera troupe.

Tā men yǎn chū de 《 hóng qiáo zèng zhū 》.
他們演出的《 虹橋贈珠 》。
Performing, "Presenting Pearl on Hongqiao Bridge."

PETER: Wǒ xǐ huān nà ge xì!
我喜歡那個戲 !
I love that one!

QIAN: Our local opera performs—

(To Cai:)

Duì bu qǐ, nà ge hóng hóng hóng shén me lái zhe—
對不起, 那個虹,虹虹什麼來著—
I'm sorry, could you please repeat—

PETER:《 Hóng qiáo zèng zhū 》.
《 虹橋贈珠 》。
"Presenting Pearl on Hongqiao Bridge."

CAI *(To Qian)*: Nǐ jìng rán méi tīng guò—
你竟然沒聽過—
You've never heard of—

(To Peter, referring to Qian:)

Kàn, xiàn zài de nián qīng rén zhēn shì!
看, 現在的年青人真是！
You see? Young people today!

QIAN: They are discussing my ignorance.

PETER: Nà duàn chàng hǎo tīng jí le—jiù shì líng bō xiān zǐ ài shàng
bái shū shēng nà duàn chàng!
那段唱好聽極了—就是凌波仙子愛上白書生那段唱！
**That beautiful aria—when fairy Lingbo admires the young
scholar!**

(Peter starts singing the aria:)

Duō xiè xiān zǐ.
多謝仙子 。
Thank you, Fairy.

(Cai joins in:)

PETER AND CAI:

Guāng huá yǒng yào qíng bù yí.

光華永燿情不移 。

This pearl shines forever like our love.

QIAN: This is what the Minister enjoys.

CAI: Zhǐ shì pái yí dìng yào zuò dé duì!

指示牌一定要做得對！

The signs must be correct!

Nà me guó jì yǒu rén jiù néng zhuān xīn xīn shǎng zhè xiē jīng jù jīng pǐn.

那麼國際友人就能專心欣賞這些京劇精品 。

So foreigners will appreciate such classic works.

QIAN: The signs must be right. Or the shows will be even worse.

DANIEL: Great! So can we talk about the deal?

PETER: Kǎ fán nuò xiān sheng tí yì jì xù tǎo lùn, hǎo ràng dà jiā hù xiāng liáo jiě.

卡凡諾先生提議繼續討論, 好讓大家互相瞭解 。

Mr. Cavanaugh would like to continue discussions, and know each other better.

CAI: Hǎo.

好 。

Good.

QIAN: Good.

XI: Wǒ hái xiáng bǔ chōng jī diǎn.

我還想補充幾點 。

I would like to add my thoughts.

QIAN: The Vice Minister would also like to speak.

XI: Yǒu guān pǔ dōng dà jù yuàn de shì qíng wǒ men zǎo zhī dào le.
有關浦東大劇院的事情我們早知道了。
We are well aware of the problems with the Pudong Grand Theatre.

QIAN: She is very familiar with the Shanghai disaster.

XI: Nà xiē xiǎo cuò wù yǐ jīng jiū zhèng guò lái le.
那些小錯誤已經糾正過來了。
These small errors have since been corrected.

QIAN: They have fixed the signs now.

XI: Wài guó rén yào xiào huà wǒ men de cuò wù hěn róng yì.
外國人要笑話我們的錯誤很容易。
It is easy for foreigners to make fun of our mistakes.

PETER: Fù jú zhǎng, wǒ men bìng bú shì yào—
副局長，我們並不是要—
Vice Minister, we were not—

XI: Kě xī fāng rén yòng zhōng wén,
可西方人用中文，
When Westerners try to use Chinese,

jié guǒ yòu rú hé ne?
結果又如何呢？
have you seen the results?

QIAN: Sometimes, Westerners try to use Chinese, too.

XI: Hàn shān shàng miàn xiě zhe「wǒ biàn tài」.
汗衫上面寫著「我變態」。
T-shirts reading: "I am pervert."

QIAN: Jumpers // which read—

PETER: Nà bú guò shì yī xiē wú zhī de lǚ kè.
那不過是一些無知的旅客 。
But those are just ignorant tourists.

(Xi produces a magazine.)

XI: Kàn zhè ge—yī běn yǒu quán wēi xìng de xué shù qī kān:
看這個—一本有權威性的學術期刊 :
Look at this—a respected Western academic journal:

mǎ kè sī pǔ lǎng kè yán jiū suǒ.
馬克思普朗克研究所 。
The Max Planck Institute.

QIAN *(Struggling to keep up)*: Um, the Vice Minister is making a comparison—

PETER *(Amused despite himself)*: Tiān na—
天哪—
Oh heavens—

XI: Tā men jué dìng zài qī kān fēng miàn yìn shàng jīng diǎn de zhōng guó shī jù.
他們決定在期刊封面印上經典的中國詩句 。
They decide to put "classic Chinese poetry" on their cover.

QIAN: Between the journal and the clothing—
DANIEL *(To Peter)*: What is she // saying?

XI: Zuì hòu tā men xuǎn shàng:
最後他們選上 :
Here's what they come up with:

PETER *(To Daniel)*: One moment. *(Looking at the magazine cover)*
Dài nǐ fā jué ré huǒ shào fù.
「 帶你發掘惹火少婦 」
"We will lead to you to young housewives with figures that will turn you on."

Bù kě sī yì!
不可思議！
Unbelievable!

DANIEL *(To Qian)*: What's that?

PETER: Yín dàng dì jiào fēng qíng
wàn zhǒng
「淫蕩地窖風情萬種」
**"These enchanting and
coquettish spring chickens will
be available in our darkened
basement."**

QIAN *(To Daniel)*:
    A magazine.
DANIEL *(To Qian)*: I know
    it's—! // Why—?
QIAN: I am attempt-
    ing to explain!
    The Vice Minister
    is—oh, this is quite
    subtle—drawing a
    comparison between
    attempts to make
    translation both
    in Western and in
    China, also pointing
    out the absurdity
    of both cultures'
    attempts to—

Tài kě xiào le!
太可笑了！
So funny!

Gāo xīn nán rén huān yíng tàn
fǎng.
「高薪男人歡迎探訪」
**"Visit us now, all men of high
incomes."**

Zhuàng yáng chūn yào yuán
yuán sòng shàng.
「壯陽春藥源源送上」
**"We can also supply to you the
elixir of Viagra."**

DANIEL: Never mind—
    what are they talk-
    ing about *now*?

XI: Tā men kān dēng le shàng hǎi yè
    zǒng huì de guǎng gào cí!
    他們刊登了上海夜總會的廣
    告詞！
    **They pulled some ad off a
    girlie bar in Shanghai!**

QIAN: Shanghai sex clubs!

> *(Pause. All look to Qian.)*
>   *To Xi and Cai:)*

> Duì bu qǐ, wó zhǐ shì xiǎng—
> 對不起, 我只是想—
> **Forgive me, I was just trying to—**

XI *(To Qian)*: Bié fèi jìng le.
别費勁了。
Don't even bother.

> *(To Peter and Daniel:)*

> Wǒ rèn wéi, wǒ men bù xū yào jí yú qǐng wài guó rén
> 我認為, 我們不需要急於請外國人
> **My point is, we must not be so quick to turn to foreigners**

> lái jiě jué wǒ men guó jiā de wèn tí.
> 來解決我們國家的問題。
> **to solve our nation's problems.**

QIAN: Foreigners are not the answer to China's problems.
DANIEL: I think we've gotten off track here. If I in any way offended //
the Minister and—

PETER: Qǐng ràng wǒ men jiě shì yí xià gāng cái de wù huì.
請讓我們解釋一下剛才的誤會。
We want to correct any wrong impressions we have made.

CAI: Hǎo le,
好了,
Please,

zhè shì rang wǒ lái chú lǐ.

這事讓我來處理 。

allow me to settle this matter.

QIAN: The Minister will now share his view.

CAI: Wǒ de kàn fǎ shì—

我的看法是—

In my opinion—

(His cell phone rings. He answers.)

Wèi?

喂 ？

Hello?

Bù, lái wǒ men guì yáng ba, bǎo zhèng nǐ men huì gèng gāo xìng!

不, 來我們貴陽吧, 保證你們會更高興 ！

No, your group will be much happier here in Guiyang!

Wǒ men zhè ge chéng shì bú dà, zhí yǒu sì bǎi wàn rén kǒu!

我們這個城市不大, 只有四百萬人口 ！

We are a small city, only four million!

Ér wǒ men nà xiē shǎo shù mín zú—dòng zú, miáo zú yā tā men—

而我們那些少數民族—侗族 、苗族呀他們—

And our minorities—the Dong and the Miao—

huì wéi nǐ men gāo xìng dì chàng gē, dào jiǔ.

會為你們高興地唱歌 、倒酒 。

sing happy songs and pour wine down your throat.

Hěn xī yǐn shì ba? Wǒ men zài tán ba.

很吸引是吧 ？我們再談吧 。

Sounds good, huh? We'll talk.

(He hangs up. To Daniel:)

Jì xù ba.
繼續吧 。
Go on.

(He shoots a look at Qian.)

QIAN: Continue.
DANIEL: Me? Um, the Minister was about to tell us . . .

CAI *(Remembering where they were)*: Duì yú nǐ gāng cái de yán lùn,
wǒ bìng méi yǒu shēng qì.
對於你剛才的言論, 我並沒有生氣 。
I take no offense at your presentation.

QIAN: He is not offended by your talk.

CAI: Fù jú zhǎng yǒu shí hòu huì yǒu yī dián gǎn qíng yòng shì.
副局長有時候會有一點感情用事 。
The Vice Minister can be very passionate.

QIAN: Madame Xi is a woman—she is emotional.

CAI: Zhè zhóng tǎn shuài de měi guó fēng gé, wǒ xīn shǎng.
這種坦率的美國風格, 我欣賞 。
I appreciate the frank American style.

QIAN: He enjoys your rudeness.
DANIEL: Um, thank you, Minister. We only want to help.
XI: Foreigner always saying to help.
QIAN: That is what foreigners . . . always . . .

(Qian doesn't know whether or not to translate.)

CAI: Xiàn zài, wǒ gēn fù jú zhǎng yào cān jiā lìng yí ge huì yì.
现在, 我跟副局長要參加另一個會議 。
Now, the Vice Minister and I have another meeting to attend.

QIAN: Now, they must continue to their next meeting.

CAI: Wǒ huì zài gēn nǐ shāng liáng jì huà shū de xì jié.
我會再跟你商量計劃書的細節 。
I want to discuss the details of your proposal.

QIAN: They will discuss your proposal further.

PETER: Kǎ fán nuò xiān sheng hái huì zài guì yáng duō liú jǐ ge xīng qī.
卡凡諾先生還會在貴陽多留幾個星期 。
Mr. Cavanaugh will remain in Guiyang for several more weeks.

CAI: Yào bu wǎn fàn zài tán?
要不晚飯再談？
Perhaps over dinner?

PETER *(To Daniel)*: Dinner?
DANIEL: Thank you. I would like that. A lot.

QIAN *(To Cai)*: Tā dā ying.
他答應 。
He accepts.

CAI *(To Daniel)*: Xiè xie.
謝謝 。
Thank you.

QIAN: Thank you.
DANIEL *(To Cai)*: No, thank you.

QIAN: Xiè xie.
謝謝 。
Thank you.

PETER *(To Cai)*: Wǒ men gōng sī huì dǎ diàn huà gēn nín zài yuē shí jiān.

我們公司會打電話跟您再約時間 。

My office will call you to arrange a time.

CAI *(To Peter)*: Nǐ gōng sī?

你公司 ？

Your office?

PETER: Wǒ huì qīn zì gěi nín dǎ diàn huà.

我會親自給您打電話 。

I'll call you.

(Daniel shakes Xi's hand.)

DANIEL *(To Xi)*: I hope you'll come to dinner, too, Vice Minister. Really.

(Xi nods.)

QIAN *(To Daniel and Peter)*: I will show you to the way out.

(Qian, Daniel and Peter exit.)

CAI *(To Xi)*: Wǒ jué dé tǐng shùn lì de, nǐ rèn wéi ne?

我覺得挺順利的, 你認為呢 ？

I think that went well, don't you?

XI: Wǒ rèn wéi wǒ men gāi zhǎo yí gè xīn de kǒu yì yuán.

我認為我們該找一個新的口譯員 。

I think we should get a new translator.

Scene 4

A restaurant frequented by locals. Xi sits at a table, with Daniel and Peter standing.

XI: <We> talk.

PETER: Dāng rán. Kǎ fán nuò xiān sheng hěn gāo xìng yǒu jī huì ké
yǐ xiāo chú xiān qián de wù huì—
當然。卡凡諾先生很高興有機會可以消除先前的誤會—
**Certainly. Mr. Cavanaugh welcomes the opportunity to clear
up any misunder—**

XI: No. Um. Only you <Daniel> and I.
PETER: Oh.
DANIEL: Alone?
XI: Hah? Yes. Alone. Only <us two.>

PETER: Nà wèi qián xiáo jiě ne?
那位錢小姐呢?
And Miss Qian?

XI: Ō, qián xiáo jiě. Nǐ shì shuō—
噢, 錢小姐。你是說—
Oh, Miss Qian. You mean the—

PETER: Nà wèi kǒu yì yuán.
那位口譯員。
The translator.

XI: Wǒ men bǎ tā sòng qù zài jiào yù le.
我們把她送去再教育了。
We sent her away to reeducation camp.

(Pause.)

Kāi wán xiào! Zhè shì gè wán xiào!
開玩笑!這是個玩笑!
Joke! It's a joke!

PETER: Wǒ míng bai. Fēi cháng yǒu qù.
我明白。非常有趣。
I knew that. Very funny.

XI: So. Better, not? Have the translator the human?

PETER: Yes, but let me understand this.
Cài jú zhǎng tā—
蔡局長他—
Minister Cai—

XI: Tā bù lái le.
他不來了。
He's not coming.

PETER: Zhè yàng a.
這樣啊。
I see.

(To Daniel:)

The Minister is not coming tonight.
XI: Apologize. But—

(Pause.)

Tā tū rán yǒu gōng wù yào chú lǐ.
他突然有公務要處理。
He is unexpectedly delayed.

PETER: I see . . .
XI: So. Well. There.

(To Peter:)

Nǐ xiàn zài ké yí zǒu le.
你現在可以走了。
Now, you are free to go.

DANIEL *(To Peter)*: It's OK.

PETER: It's just that // —you see, we never—
DANIEL: I think it's a great idea. For the Vice Minister and I to talk on our own.

(To Xi:)

Just us two. Straighten this all out.
PETER: Well, all right, then. I'll // just leave . . .
DANIEL: Go on, we'll be fine!
PETER: I'll be next door. In the karaoke bar. On my mobile. If anything changes, if you need anything, anything at all, // you just—
DANIEL: Go!
PETER: Mobile.
DANIEL: Cluck, cluck, cluck.
XI *(To Peter)*: <What's he talking about?>
DANIEL *(To Xi)*: Mother hen. Cluck, cluck, cluck.
XI *(To Peter)*: <I still don't get it.>
PETER *(To Xi)*: Ku, ku, ku.
XI: Ah!

(To Peter:)

Mǔ jī!
母雞 !
Mother hen!

(To Daniel:)

Ku, ku, ku.
PETER: Cheers!

(Peter exits. Silence, then:)

DANIEL: Your English . . .
XI: So.
DANIEL: I didn't realize, until the end of the meeting, that you . . .

(Silence.)

Speak. English.

XI: Ah! I, um, live. Outside. China. For am, six year, ah, no, month. Six month. Outside. Therefore, ah. Study.

DANIEL: You've lived abroad.

XI: Study the English.

DANIEL: In the States.

(Pause.)

XI: Hah?

DANIEL: You lived? In the States?

XI: In—? Ah, no, no.

DANIEL: Because you seemed to know something about Cleveland. So—where . . . ? Where did. You live?

XI: Here. Guiyang.

DANIEL: No, before. When you lived // abroad.

XI: Ah! Sri Lanka.

DANIEL: Sri Lanka.

XI: Foreign-exchange student.

DANIEL: Great. Well, I really appreciate this opportunity, Ms. Xi. To sit down, one on one. Clear up any misunderstanding that hangs over our—

XI: Too fast speed.

DANIEL: Sorry, // I didn't—

XI: Only two. So therefore. Talking not so much necessary.

DANIEL: I couldn't agree with you // more.

XI: Also, very, um, sleepy.

(Pause.)

Sleepy? Sleeping? Sleeper?

DANIEL: You're sleepy.

XI: You sleepy.

DANIEL: I'm sleepy.

XI: When so fast the words. Sleepy.

DANIEL: Before talking business, we should order, don't you think? *(Picking up menu)* Order. Food.

XI: Dáo xiǎng kàn kan.
倒想看看 。
I'd like to see that.

(Daniel peruses the menu. It's in Chinese. He puts it down.)

I order the past.
DANIEL: You—already ordered?
XI: Yes.
DANIEL: Good! No need for me to . . . to . . .

XI: huāng zhāng.
慌張 。
panic.

DANIEL *(Attempting to imitate her)*: kuā zhāng.
誇張 。
splat.

(Xi looks away.)

I'm trying! <Thumbs-up.>

XI: Zhēn zāo gāo.
真糟糕 。
That's the sad part. <Thumbs-up.>

DANIEL: Ms. Xi. Vice Minister. The fact that Minister Cai. Sent you.
Instead of coming himself. I gotta say, I read something into that.
Something. Not so good. But I believe we can get past that.

(Pause.)

Right?

xı: Tīng bù dǒng.
聽不懂 。
Didn't catch a word.

DANIEL: Wow. OK. Minister Cai—
xı: Cai.
DANIEL: Cai? He seems. Friendly. To my proposal.
xı: "Proposal"?
DANIEL: My deal. For my company. To make the English signs. For
    the // Cultural Center.
xı: Ah yes.
DANIEL: Deal.
xı: Yes.
DANIEL: Cai.
xı: Yes.
DANIEL: He likes.
xı: No.
DANIEL: Cai—does *not* like my deal.
xı: Yes.

> *(Pause.)*

Shì zhè yàng de.
是這樣的 。
Here's the thing.

Nǐ yǐ wéi tā xǐ huān nǐ de jiàn yì,
你以為他喜歡你的建議,
You think he likes your offer,

qí shí nǐ nòng cuò le.
其實你弄錯了 。
but you're wrong.

Shì tā pài wǒ lái zhè lǐ de,
是他派我來這裡的,
Which is why he sent me to meet you here.

Cái yǒu xiàn zài zhè qí guài de chǎng miàn.

才有現在這奇怪的場面 。

Under these impossible conditions.

DANIEL: OK, I have a very strong feeling what you said to me is really important. So. Please. Repeat. In English.

XI: Such sleepy.

(Pause.)

You believing. Cai. Your deal has friendly. No. Cai disassemble.

DANIEL: "Disassemble"?

XI: Qí mǎ yīng yǔ tīng dé dǒng ba!

起碼英語聽得懂吧！

At least keep up with the English!

DANIEL: Dissembling. He's lying?

XI: Yes! Lie! But. Cannot tell to the Teacher.

DANIEL: Who's the Teacher?

XI: Āi yā, zhēn yào mìng!

哎呀, 真要命！

Oh, for crying out loud!

(Trying ever harder to make him understand:)

English, the Teacher! Teacher Peter!

DANIEL: Peter. My consultant?

XI: Teacher Peter!

DANIEL: He *used* to teach, I think. But now he is. A consultant.

XI: Consultant, consultant. Everyone name. But nothing doing.

DANIEL: He's *not* a consultant?

XI: Nothing. Now, what explanation, you cannot say.

DANIEL: OK . . .

XI: "Use at your own risk."

(Xi leans in, whispers to Daniel:)

English-writing firm. Currently enter. Through the back door.
Cai wife sister. Open door. So will not close.

(Pause.)

Now, you know.

(Pause.)

DANIEL: Could you repeat that?

XI: "Repeat"?
Jiù píng gāng cái zhè xiē huà, dōu gòu wǒ qiāng bì de le!
就憑剛才這些話, 都夠我槍斃的了！
For what I just told you, I could be shot!

Nǐ hái yào wǒ zài shuō yī biàn?
你還要我再說一遍？
You want me to say that again?

Jiù pà wàn yī yǒu rén méi tīng qīng shì ba?
就怕萬一有人沒聽清是吧？
In case anyone else in the room missed it?

DANIEL: I understand. That what you're telling me is a huge—use at
your own risk.
XI: Yes! Use at your own risk!
DANIEL: But I— <have no idea—>
XI: OK, OK . . . *(Leans in again)* English-writing firm . . .
DANIEL: The company making the English signs . . .
XI: In present . . .
DANIEL: Um, presently?
XI: Enter through the back door. Of Minister wife sister.

(Silence.)

Wǒ kuài bèi nǐ qì fēng le.
我快被你氣瘋了。
I'm going to shoot myself.

DANIEL: Give me a chance here. "Minister wife sister." Cai's sister-in-law?

XI: Yes . . .

DANIEL: Is presently hired—to make the signs?

XI: Yes! Through the back door!

DANIEL: That's the part that keeps tripping me up. But—OK, then, why does Minister Cai— Why Cai pretend. Pretend? Why Cai pretend— He like my deal?

XI: Ah. Good. Because. English Teacher.

DANIEL: Peter . . .

XI: Also open back door.

DANIEL: We're back to that.

XI: For university Bath. Cai son.

(Pause.)

Zhè yǐ jīng hěn míng xiǎn le!
這已經很明顯了！
This is so obvious!

DANIEL: What is "caisson"?

XI: Son! Son! Like, ah, daughter, but // son!

DANIEL: Oh! Cai's son. Cai has a son!

XI: Yes! In Bath!

DANIEL: And English Teacher Peter . . . got Cai's son . . . to some university for a bath?

XI: Bath! Is City! In England!

DANIEL: Oh, "Bath" is a city!

XI: With university!

DANIEL: Peter got Cai's son into a university in England?

XI: Yes! Through back door!

DANIEL: Cai owes Peter a favor. But Cai cannot—give the contract to Peter's client. He can't open the—back door for Peter.

XI: Yes.

DANIEL: Because he has already . . . opened it.

XI: For // his wife sister—

DANIEL: His sister-in-law! I got it, I got it!

XI: High-five!

(They high-five.)

DANIEL: That was exhausting.

XI: I am sleeping with you.

(Pause.)

Sleepy? Sleeper?

(Pause.)

In talking? Such the manner? <Wears you out.>

DANIEL: You mean, it's tiring. To talk like this. // Tiring.

XI: Yes. We sleep together.

DANIEL: That's not what you mean.

(Pause.)

Unless . . .

(Pause.)

So. You tell me. Cai is. Against me. Because Peter goes. Through Cai's back door.

XI: No. Cai go through Peter back door.

DANIEL: Right, right. So am I just—screwed?

(Xi laughs.)

XI: Lǎo sè láng.
老色狼 。
Dirty old man.

DANIEL: Oh, that? That you know? You know "screwed"?
XI: All person know "screwed"!
DANIEL: *Am* I screwed?

XI: Wǒ bù zhī dào.
我不知道 。
I don't know.

Ní xiǎng ma?
你想嗎 ?
Do you want to be?

DANIEL: No, stop that. When you break into Chinese // I get completely—
XI: You not screw. Cai send me see you. Telling you no deal. Go away!
DANIEL: He sent you to tell me no deal.
XI: But. *I* thinking. Good, your deal.
DANIEL: So instead, you're going to—help me?
XI: Mmmm.
DANIEL: Well, thank you. Thank you so // much.
XI: But exclusive we.
DANIEL: I understand. This is all secret.
XI: Now. <Get your phone.> Mobile.
DANIEL: Oh, call Peter!
XI: English Teacher, yes! Telling, I saying you no. No deal.

(Xi gets up to leave. Daniel begins dialing his cell. Then:)

DANIEL: But—the food hasn't arrived yet. Food?
XI: Oh, I no order. <Thumbs-up!>
DANIEL: <Thumbs-up!> But why? Why are you. Helping me? Why?

(Pause.)

XI: Use at your own risk.

(She exits. Daniel watches her go. Then he dials his cell phone.
Peter enters.)

PETER: I saw her leaving. Don't worry, she didn't see me.

DANIEL: I'm not worried. I think it went—fine.

PETER: So what did she say?

DANIEL: Well . . . it was a little hard to understand.

PETER: What did you manage to grasp?

DANIEL: Well, I think she was trying to tell me . . . Why don't *you*
tell *me*?

PETER: Excuse // me?

DANIEL: I mean, you're the consultant.

PETER: Right.

DANIEL: You know the lay of the land here. Just // give it a—

PETER: Well, my guess is, that she tried to convince you—surrepti-
tiously—that the Minister had decided to reject your proposal.

DANIEL: Wow.

PETER: Am I . . . somewhere in the ballpark?

DANIEL: I'm amazed. How did you—?

PETER: It was quite clear in the room, now wasn't it? That Cai was
totally supportive of the idea. Whereas Ms. Xi—was dead set
against it.

DANIEL: That seemed pretty clear.

PETER: Ms. Xi cannot openly oppose him, however. So she tells you
that your proposal is rejected, and you go home. Suddenly, no
one has to deal with the inconvenient American.

DANIEL: Ms. Xi told me something.

PETER: Ah.

DANIEL: About your particular relationship with Cai.

PETER: That Cai owes me a favor?

DANIEL: Yeah.

PETER: It's true. I arranged for Jin—Cai's son—to be admitted to the
University of Bath. Where I taught for a while.

DANIEL: You taught.

PETER: Yes, when I was fresh out of // university . . .

DANIEL: Before you became . . .

PETER: A consultant, // yes.

DANIEL: A China consultant.

PETER: Did she tell you . . . anything else about me?

DANIEL: Like what?

PETER: Anything at all, I'm just // wondering—

DANIEL: I, I've gotta say, I don't understand, why you couldn't have told me // about that.

PETER: Yes, I // —You have every right to feel—

DANIEL: All I'm saying, is that we gotta be honest with each other.

PETER: Absolutely.

DANIEL: As partners, if we're not open, then // who—

PETER: Then who can be? It's—you're—

DANIEL: We may be dealing with the Chinese, but we can be Westerners, capiche?

PETER: Absolutely. Capiche. But, listen, here's the thing I can't understand. Why is Ms. Xi risking so much—going behind the back of her superior—to block the awarding of a single contract to a foreign firm?

DANIEL: That *is* a good // question.

PETER: I wonder about her husband.

DANIEL: Her—she's married?

PETER: Yes. Her husband is a Judge.

DANIEL: Of course // she's married.

PETER: Of the Second—or Third—Intermediate Court. These sorts of things, once you get to the bottom, often involve some sort of family connections. For all we know, he could be on the payroll of another firm bidding against us for the contract.

DANIEL: That's good.

PETER: Yes, it's something like that, I'll wager.

DANIEL: Do some research on her husband, // that's good.

PETER: The first thing I'll do is report all this to Minister Cai. This was a truly foolhardy move on her part. How could she have failed to realize that you'd report everything she said back to me?

DANIEL: Maybe she thought I was gonna get so discouraged, I'd just give up. That I'd decide it was all too hard, since I don't have a clue what's really going on here. And that my consultant couldn't actually do a thing for me, because, despite whoever's back door he ripped open at his Old Boy's Club, it hadn't given him any real power. That he couldn't get the job done, couldn't close the deal. Maybe that's what she figured I'd think.

PETER: If so, well . . . well she's wrong.

(Pause.)

She's only Cai's underling. I promise you, this deal is going to happen.

DANIEL: Good. Because I don't mind telling you, this Guanxi is pretty damned confusing.

Scene 5

Xi and Cai, in Cai's office.

CAI: Bǐ dé lǎo shī yī zhí zài géi wó dǎ diàn huà.
彼得老師一直在給我打電話 。
Teacher Peter keeps calling me.

XI: Wǒ bù zǎo shuō guò huì zhè yàng ma?
我不早說過會這樣嗎？
Didn't I tell you this would happen?

CAI: Duì měi guó rén jiù shì yào tài dù qiáng yìng.
對美國人就是要態度強硬 。
You have to be forceful with the American.

XI: Wó yǒu yā.
我有呀 。
I was.

CAI: Nà tā zěn me hái zài guì yáng?

那他怎麼還在貴陽？

Then why is he still in Guiyang?

XI: Dà gài shì bǐ dé lǎo shī gēn tā shuō—

大概是彼得老師跟他說—

Teacher Peter is probably telling him—

CAI: Bǐ dé lǎo shī, bǐ dé lǎo shī!

彼得老師、彼得老師！

Teacher Peter, Teacher Peter!

Tā bù gāi lǎo tīng bǐ dé lǎo shī de huà.

他不該老聽彼得老師的話。

He should know better than to listen to Teacher Peter.

XI: Tā yǐ wéi bǐ dé lǎo shī shì yī gè qǐ yè gù wèn.

他以為彼得老師是一個企業顧問。

He thinks Teacher Peter is a business consultant.

CAI: Ná yǒu rén zhè me bèn?

哪有人這麼笨？

How can anyone be so stupid?

XI: Shéi jiào nǐ dā yìng gěi tā bāng máng.

誰叫你答應給他幫忙？

You're the one who promised Peter a favor.

CAI: Wó yǐ wéi tā yǒu hé lǐ de yāo qiú!

我以為他有合理的要求！

I thought he would ask for something reasonable!

Xiàng zài xué xiào lí gěi tā jiàn xīn de bàn gōng shì!

像在學校裡給他建新的辦公室！

Like a new office for his school!

XI: Nà nǐ zì jǐ gēn bǐ dé shuō.
那你自己跟彼得說。
So tell Peter yourself.

CAI: Nǐ qù ba,
你去吧,
You do it,

ní bí wǒ qiáng yìng ma!
你比我強硬嘛!
you're tougher than I am!

Wó lǎo pó tā jiě bú duàn géi wó dǎ diàn huà.
我老婆她姐不斷給我打電話:
My sister-in-law keeps calling.

Wǒ men shén me shí hòu kāi shǐ wéi wén huà zhōng xīn zuò zhǐ shì pái yā?
「我們什麼時候開始為文化中心做指示牌呀?
"When can I start making the signs for the Cultural Center?"

Yào gěi gōng rén fā gōng zī de!
要給工人發工資的!」
"I have employees to pay!"

XI: Wǒ zhī dào.
我知道。
I know.

CAI: Tā zhěng tiān xiàng wó lǎo pó gào zhuàng.
她整天向我老婆告狀,
She spends all day complaining to my wife.

Gǎo dào wǒ huí jiā lǎo pó jiù yī zhí láo dāo, mán yuàn wǒ bù zhōng yòng.
搞到我回家老婆就一直嘮叨, 埋怨我不中用。
So when I get home, she nags me about how I am a bad provider.

Tā, bá wǒ dà bàn gè yuè de gōng zī ná qù shàng hái mǎi LV de
nǔ rén hái hǎo yì si shuō wǒ.

她, 把我大半個月的工資拿去上海買LV的女人還好意思說
我 。

**This, from a woman who spends more than half my monthly
salary at Louis Vuitton in Shanghai.**

XI: Jú zhǎng, zhè xiē wǒ bù xū yào zhī dào ba?

局長, 這些我不需要知道吧 ?

Minister, this is more than I need to hear.

CAI: Bié lǎo shì nà me yán sù,

別老是那麼嚴肅,

Don't be so uptight.

Nǐ lǎo gōng dà gài yě bù róng yì xiāng chǔ.

你老公大概也不容易相處 。

Your husband can't be easy to live with, either.

Shéi dōu zhī dào zhè dì fāng de gàn bù, jiù shù tā yě xīn zuì dà

誰都知道這地方的幹部, 就數他野心最大 。

**Everyone knows he's the most ambitious politician in the
province.**

XI: Nǐ duì wó lǎo gōng yī wú suǒ zhī!

你對我老公一無所知 !

You know nothing about my husband!

Tā rén hěn zhèng zhí—duì wǒ, duì ér zi dōu hěn hǎo.

他人很正直—對我 、對兒子都很好 。

He behaves with such integrity—to me, and our son.

CAI: Hǎo ba. Bú gào sù wǒ jiù suàn le.

好吧, 不告訴我就算了 。

Fine. You don't have to tell me.

Bú guò wǒ quàn ní zhǎo gè shén me rén shuō shuo.
不過我勸你找個什麼人說說 。
But you should talk to *someone*.

XI: Nín bì xū qīn zì jù jué bǐ dé!
您必須親自拒絕彼得 ！
You need to say no to Peter yourself!

CAI: Wó yǒu gèng zhòng yào de shì qíng yào chú lǐ!
我有更重要的事情要處理 ！
I have bigger problems to deal with!

Shěng wěi shū ji jīn tiān géi wó dǎ diàn huà,
省委書記今天給我打電話,
The Party Secretary called today,

wèn wó dǎ suàn rú hé xī yǐn gèng duō yóu kè!
問我打算如何吸引更多遊客 ！
asking how I plan to attract more tourists!

XI: Nà jiù gǎo xiē jì huà ràng shū jì gāo xìng gāo xìng.
那就搞些計劃讓書記高興高興 。
So make the Secretary happy.

Ān pái nà xiē zhōng guó zá jì tuán lái biáo yǎn yī xià.
安排那些中國雜技團來表演一下 。
Schedule a performance by the Chinese Acrobats.

CAI: Bù! Wǒ zuì tǎo yàn zhōng guó zá jì.
不 ！我最討厭中國雜技 。
Never! I loathe the Chinese Acrobats.

Yī gè rén liàn jǐ shí nián zhǐ shì wèi le yào zài bí zi shàng dǐng
zhù yī bá yǐ zi.
一個人練幾十年只是為了要在鼻子上頂住一把椅子 。
A man spends decades learning to balance a chair on his nose.

Wǒ zhēn xiǎng gào sù tā,
我真想告訴他,
I want to say to him,

gē mén, nǐ zhè bèi zi bái huó le!
哥們, 你這輩子白活了！
"Buddy, you just wasted your whole life!"

XI: Jú zhǎng, zuò rén yào yǔ shí bìng jìn.
局長, 做人要與時並進。
Minister, you have to change with the times.

CAI: Nà yě bù děng yú shén me dōu yào xiàng qián kàn ba?
那也不等於什麼都要向錢看吧？
Does that mean everything now has to make money?

Yǒu shí hòu wǒ hái zhēn huái niàn bù duì shí dài de shēng huó.
有時候我還真懷念部隊時代的生活。
Sometimes I miss my old army days.

XI: Shì ma? Nán dào nǐ huái niàn wén huà dà gé mìng?
是嗎? 難道你懷念文化大革命？
Oh, really? You miss the Cultural Revolution?

CAI: Zhì shǎo nà ge nián dài, bǐ jiào dān chún.
至少那個年代, 比較單純。
At least, times were simpler then.

Nǐ qù jiě jué bǐ dé lǎo shī de wèn tí,
你去解決彼得老師的問題,
***You* take care of Teacher Peter.**

Nà shì nǐ de gōng zuò.
那是你的工作。
That's your job.

XI: Nà hǎo ba, lǐng dǎo tóng zhì.

那好吧, 領導同志 。

As you wish, Comrade.

(Xi exits.)

Scene 6

The lobby restaurant of Daniel's hotel. He is sitting at the bar with Xi.

XI: Important. I again telling you go. Yet, again, you stay.

DANIEL: I—*should* stay?

XI: Yes. Until Minister Cai, himself, saying, "No deal!"

DANIEL: Then no deal?

XI: No. Then deal! Hooray!

DANIEL: I don't think I'm quite // following this . . .

XI: You not telling to the Teacher, correct?

DANIEL: Peter. That you're helping me? No.

XI: Good. I not tell nobody, I here now. Not Cai, not husband.

DANIEL: Your husband. Yes, I heard you were— What does your husband do?

XI: He is perfect.

DANIEL: Oh, that's great, but // what I meant—

XI: Qí shí tā hén tǎo yàn.

其實他很討厭 。

Actually, he can be a real jerk.

DANIEL: Excuse me?

XI: Zì wǒ zhōng xīn.

自我中心 。

Self-centered.

Hěn má fan.

很麻煩 。

A pain in the ass.

DANIEL: You're—I—can't understand.

XI: I know!

(Pause.)

Yǒu yì si.

有意思 。

This is interesting.

DANIEL: I meant. What does he do? For work? Your husband—his job?

XI: Ah. He is Judge.

DANIEL: Strange to be a Judge—

XI: Yes, // strange.

DANIEL: —in a country with no real judicial system.

XI: Tā zěn qù shěn pàn bié rén ne?

他怎去審判別人呢？

How can he judge others?

Zài jiā lǐ, tā jiǎn zhí shì méi tóu méi nǎo de.

在家裡, 他簡直是沒頭沒腦的 。

At home, he's totally clueless.

DANIEL: OK, what are you trying to tell me?

XI: Hah?

DANIEL: You speak. Chinese. And it's important. I can see that. In
    your face. So—what do you want to say?

(Pause.)

XI: My husband—sometimes . . . not so perfect.

DANIEL: See? That wasn't so hard, was it? My wife—if I started to tell you! . . . My wife and I: Really. Not perfect.

XI: My husband, only thinking himself, so therefore, no understanding.

DANIEL: And he doesn't know you're here?

XI: He not ask.

DANIEL: The two of you don't—talk so much? No talking?

XI: Is better, agree? Husband and wife, not so much, talk?

DANIEL: Wow. Back home, that isn't really a // philosophy—

XI: Making the long marriage. You, your wife—talk?

DANIEL: Do we—? Well, since I've been here in China. With the time difference. Day is night, night is day.

XI: Yes. Husband, wife. Day, night. We agree.

DANIEL: I guess. And you're OK with that? You want that?

XI *(Laughs, then)*: Shéi huì zài hu ne?
誰會在乎呢？
Nobody ever asks.

(She rises to leave.)

So. You wait. For Cai say, no deal.

DANIEL: Then, hooray?

XI: Full marks!

(She starts to go, then:)

DANIEL: Ms. Xi. Why are you helping me?

(Pause.)

Why are you going behind your boss's back? Your husband's back, if I understand this correctly? For—what? A foreigner, some guy you just met? Are perfectly translated signs so important to you, that you would risk so much?

(Pause.)

Got that off my chest. Don't expect you to understand.

XI: Why? Because you—are good.

DANIEL: I'm good? You—you don't even know me.

XI: Kě xìn.
可信 。
Credible.

Kě kào.
可靠 。
Trustworthy.

(Pause.)

Honest. Good man.

(Pause.)

DANIEL: Wow. You can't possibly—you have no idea—how long it's been since someone said that to—thought // —showed that kind of—

XI: Your face.

DANIEL: My . . . face?

XI: Good face.

(Pause. They look into each other's eyes.)

DANIEL: You're doing all this because—my face is—?

XI: Jiù xiàng nǐ rén shēng zǒng shì yī fán fēng shùn,
就像你人生總是一帆風順,
Like your life has been easy.

Suó yí nǐ néng bǎo chí chún zhēn.

所以你能保持純真 。

And you still have your innocence.

Honest.

(Pause.)

DANIEL: Well, I . . . I am. Honest. I'm not saying I'm— But maybe,
over here, where there's so much—secrecy. At least I'm sincere.
I try. To tell the truth.

XI: Truth, yes.
Dàn yuàn wǒ de rén shēng yǒu gèng duō.
但願我的人生有更多 。
I wish I had more of that in my life.

(Pause.)

I like.

DANIEL: I come here—all the way across and—and I feel so—lost.
Then you appear. And tell me . . . I'm good.

(Pause.)

Your face. Is—so beautiful.

XI: My—? No. Nose, too—

DANIEL: Oh c'mon, look at you, you're perfect.

XI: Perfect?
Zhēn de?
真的 ？
Really?

DANIEL: And not just on the outside, but, I think—your heart . . .

XI: My—heart?

DANIEL: On the inside—too.

XI: Nǐ kàn zhe wǒ de yǎn shén, jiù xiàng . . .
　　你看著我的眼神, 就像……
　　The way you look at me . . .

(Daniel leans in, kisses her, then immediately pulls back.)

DANIEL: I'm sorry, I—that was really out of—forgive me, I—

(She slaps him.)

　　Yes, I deserve—

XI: Number.

DANIEL: You're absolutely—I // am so—

XI: Room. Number. *(Loudly)* Asshole!

(She starts to leave.)

DANIEL: Um, 803.

XI: Stay. Then go.
　　(Loudly) Cào ní zǔ zōng shí bā dài!
　　操你祖宗十八代！
　　Fuck your ancestors to the eighteenth generation!

(She exits. A Waitress stares at Daniel.)

DANIEL: Check?

(Crossfade to a tight spot on Xi's face.)

XI: Nǐ hái zhēn xíng.

你還真行。

You are a good fuck.

Wó lǎo gōng yǐ qián yé hěn xíng,

我老公以前也很行,

Of course, my husband was a good fuck, too.

Jiù shì wǒ men gāng rèn shí de shí hòu,

就是我們剛認識的時候,

When we first met.

Bù guǎn zài nár wǒ men dōu néng dà gàn yī chǎng,

不管在哪兒我們都能大幹一場,

Oh, we would fuck everyplace.

Yóu qí wǎn shàng zài gōng yuán lǐ.

尤其晚上在公園裡。

Especially in the park at night.

Zài nà ge shí hòu, nà xiē hái gēn jiā lǐ rén zhù de nián qīng nán nǚ dōu dào gōng yuán qù.

在那個時候, 那些還跟家裡人住的年青男女都到公園去。

In those days, all the young couples still living at home went to the park.

Wǒ kàn bú dào tā de liǎn,

我看不到他的臉,

I couldn't see his face,

wǒ men shèn zhì méi yǒu fā chū rèn hé shēng yīn.

我們甚至沒有發出任何聲音。

and we didn't say a word.

Dàn shì zài tuō xià wǒ chèn yī de shí hòu,

但是在脫下我襯衣的時候,

but his fingers trembled,

tā de shóu zhǐ yī zhí zài fā dǒu.
他的手指一直在發抖 。
as he undid my blouse.

Zài xǔ duō rén xīn mù zhōng,
在許多人心目中,
To everyone else,

tā yōu xiù, shàng jìn.
他優秀 、上進 。
he was smart and ambitious.

Kě gēn wǒ zài gōng yuán de shí hòu,
可跟我在公園的時候,
But in the park with me,

tā huì xiàng shēng háo yī yàng dǎ kāi,
他會像生蠔一樣打開,
he broke open like an oyster,

duì wó zhǎn shì tā suó yǒu de yù wàng.
對我展示他所有的慾望 。
and showed me all his need.

Tā yòng zuǐ ba jín jǐn hán zhù wǒ de rǔ fáng,
他用嘴巴緊緊合住我的乳房,
His lips closed around my breast,

jiù xiàng wǒ néng wèi tā tí gōng shēng mìng,
就像我能為他提供生命,
as if I could give him life itself,

zhè ràng wó gǎn jué dào yī zhǒng shēn qíng,
這讓我感覺到一種深情,
making me feel so much in love,

yī zhǒng qián suǒ wèi yǒu de, shēn qíng.

一種前所未有的, 深情 。

and more powerful than I ever dreamed possible.

(Lights reveal Xi and Daniel in his hotel room, she in his arms, postcoital.)

DANIEL: The first time we met? I thought you despised me.

XI: Yes!

DANIEL: No. Despise. Hate me. Did you?

XI: Bié yào wǒ shuō huà, tài lèi rén le.

別要我說話, 太累人了 。

Don't ask me to talk, it's too much work.

DANIEL: Why do you speak Chinese? When you know I can't understand a word?

(Pause.)

Why you? Speak Chinese?

XI: I am Chinese.

DANIEL: Good point.

(Pause.)

Well, understand this: You are so beautiful. *(He kisses her)*

XI: Ah. Better. *(She kisses him back)*

DANIEL: When we met, did you ever dream we'd end up . . . ?

(Pause.)

XI: Wǒ jì dé zhè zhǒng shí kè,

我記得這種時刻,

I remember this moment,

tā kàn jìn ní yán lǐ, yī rán zhǎo dào wán měi.

他看進你眼裡, 依然找到完美 。

when he looks into your eyes, and still sees perfection.

DANIEL: Well, I sure didn't. Then I found out you're married. And I figured any husband of yours must be crazy in love with you.

XI: Hah?

DANIEL: You're right, let's not talk about your . . .

XI: My husband? I? Love—? <The idea makes me shudder.>

DANIEL: You don't love your husband?

XI: Once—long time—but, no. Today, only husband.

DANIEL: Then why don't you . . . you know, break up? Escape your marriage?

XI: Yes, escape. But. Not so easy.

DANIEL: You mean, here. In China. Marriage is hard to—?

XI: Not so easy.

(Pause.)

DANIEL: I've thought about that, too. Leaving my—to be honest, I think about it all the time. But I've never—not like you. You're not afraid to just . . . come out and say it.

(Pause.)

It's crazy, but I—I feel like you know me.

(Pause.)

XI: Talk. More.

DANIEL: Like you can somehow see—into my heart. The me I want to be, that I can be, the real me. Honest man.

XI: Honest man.

(Pause.)

Nǐ shuō huà ba, wǒ jiù ài kàn zhe nǐ de zuǐ chún dòng.

你說話吧, 我就愛看著你的嘴唇動 。

When you speak, I love to watch your lips move.

(They kiss.)

Scene 7

Cai answers his cell phone.

CAI: Wèi?

喂 ?

Hello?

Bǐ dé lǎo shī?

彼得老師 ?

Teacher Peter?

Ní zěn zhī dào zhè ge hào mǎ?

你怎知道這個號碼 ?

How did you get this—?

Yǒu, dāng rán yǒu!

有, 當然有 !

Yes, of course!

Wǒ jiù zhǔn bèi géi nǐ huí diàn—

我就準備給你回電—

I've been meaning to call you about—

Dāng rán ké yǐ!

當然可以 !

Of course!

Míng tiān hǎo ma? Zhōng wǔ ba?
明天好嗎？中午吧？
How about tomorrow? Noon?

Hǎo, nà míng tiān jiàn!
好, 那明天見！
Looking forward!

(Crossfade to Cai's office. Cai, Xi, Peter, Daniel and Bing, a male in his twenties, the new translator, are there.)

Shì shí shàng, wǒ zhèng chéng shòu zhe chén zhòng de yā lì.
事實上, 我正承受著沈重的壓力 。
The fact is, I am under a great deal of pressure.

BING: The Minister is underneath you.

CAI: Shéng wěi shū jì yǒu tā de yì xiàng wǒ néng zuò shén me ne?
省委書記有他的意向, 我能做什麼呢？
The Party Secretary has his priorities, so what can I do?

BING: He also underneath his Party Secretary.

CAI: Wǒ shù shǒu wú cè!
我束手無策！
My hands are tied!

BING: He is in bondage.

PETER: Jú zhǎng, hén gǎn xiè nín de jiē jiàn, dàn nín de yì si shì—
局長, 很感謝您的接見, 但您的意思是—
Minister, we are grateful for this meeting, but are you saying—?

CAI: Bǐ dé lǎo shī, zhè fèn jì huà shū wǒ bù néng pī.
彼得老師, 這份計劃書我不能批 。
Teacher Peter, I cannot approve this proposal.

BING: He cannot fulfill your desires.

PETER: Shén me?
什麼？
What?

CAI: Wó hěn bào qiàn.
我很抱歉。
I am so sorry.

DANIEL: What's going on, here?

PETER: Wǒ men bú shì gōu tōng hǎo de ma!
我們不是溝通好的嗎！
But we had an understanding!

CAI: Wǒ huì lǚ xíng wǒ de chéng nuò! Xià yí cì ba!
我會履行我的承諾！下一次吧！
And I will honor our agreement! Another time!

BING *(To Daniel)*: Next time, he may give it to you.

PETER: Dàn shì nǐ dā ying guò, nǐ shuō—
但是你答應過, 你說—
But you promised, you said—!

CAI: Wǒ bù néng bá zhǐ shì pái de hé yuē pī géi kǎ fán nuò xiān sheng!
我不能把指示牌的合約批給卡凡諾先生！
I cannot give Mr. Cavanaugh the signage contract!

Wó hěn bào qiàn!
我很抱歉！
I'm very sorry!

Qíng ní lí jiě.
請你理解。
You understand.

DANIEL *(To Peter)*: What's he saying?

BING: Teacher Peter begs the Minister for his favors—

DANIEL *(To Bing)*: It's OK.

     (To Peter, regarding Bing) This guy's even worse than the last one.

BING: Oh! Rudeness!

PETER *(To Daniel)*: The Minister has rejected your proposal.

CAI: Sorry.

DANIEL: Well, I'm disappointed to hear that.

BING: Nǐ tīng dào nà lǎo wài zěn yàng wú rú wǒ ma?

你聽到那老外怎樣侮辱我嗎？

Did you hear that foreigner insult me?

DANIEL *(Prompting for translation)*: Peter?

BING *(To Cai)*: Jiù jiu?

舅舅？

Uncle?

(Cai shushes Bing.)

PETER: Duì yú zhè yàng tū rán de gǎi biàn kǎ fán nuò xiān sheng shí fēn shī wàng.

對於這樣突然的改變卡凡諾先生十分失望。

Mr. Cavanaugh is extremely disappointed by this sudden change of course.

CAI: Dàn nǐ néng lí jiě ba?

但你能理解吧？

But you understand?

PETER: Shì de. Dāng rán.

是的。當然。

Yes. Of course.

Xiè xie nín, jú zhǎng.
謝謝您, 局長 。
Thank you, Minister.

(Cai stands, prompting the others. They shake hands all around. Peter stands apart.)

DANIEL *(To Cai)*: Who knows? Maybe we'll do something else together.

BING: Wǒ huì gào sù wǒ mā é.
我會告訴我媽哦 。
My mother will hear about this.

CAI *(To Bing)*: Ràng wǒ qù gào sù tā!
讓我去告訴她 !
Yes, she will!

DANIEL: Peter! <Get over here.>

CAI *(To Daniel)*: Zhù nǐ yí lù shùn fēng.
祝你一路順風 。
Travel home safely.

BING *(To Daniel)*: Leave in haste!

(Daniel moves to Xi.)

DANIEL: Vice Minister, it has been a pleasure.

BING: Nǐ kàn! Zhè lǎo wài mù guāng wéi suǒ.
你看 ! 這老外目光猥瑣 。
Look! This white devil has lust in his eyes.

XI: Thank you.
DANIEL: C'mon, Peter, let's—

PETER: No! Bù! Wǒ bù míng bái!
不！我不明白！
No, I do not understand!

Nǐ dā yìng guò de! Nǐ duì wǒ shuō,
你答應過的！你對我說：
You promised! You said to me,

"Zhǐ yào nǐ néng bāng wǒ ér zi, wú lùn nǐ yào shén me, wǒ dōu
huì shí xiàn tā."
「只要你能幫我兒子，無論你要什麼，我都會實現它。」
**"If you can only do this for my son, whatever you ask, I will
make it happen."**

CAI: Zài hé lǐ de qíng kuàng xià!
在合理的情況下！
Within reason!

PETER: Hé lǐ?
合理？
Reason?

Nǐ rèn wéi nà yòu hé lǐ ma?
你認為那又合理嗎？
You think it was reasonable?

Bá nǐ de ér zi sòng jìn bā sī dà xué?
把你的兒子送進巴斯大學？
To get your son admitted to Bath?

Nà xiǎo zi jiǎn zhí shì jiào yù jiè de zāi nàn!
那小子簡直是教育界的災難！
That boy is an educational disaster zone!

CAI: Nǐ yīng gāi zhī dào—
你應該知道—
You should know—!

PETER: Wǒ zhī dào! Yīn wèi wǒ shì tā de yīng yú dǎo shī!
我知道！因為我是他的英語導師！
I do know! I was his English tutor!

Shàng le sān nián háo wú yì yì de kè,
上了三年毫無意義的課，
After three years of pointless lessons,

tā wéi yī xué huì de yīng yǔ jiù shì:
他唯一學會的英語就是：
the only English he learned was:

"My Father is a big Party official."

CAI: Gòu le! Zhè lǐ de rén bù xiǎng tīng dào—
夠了！這裡的人不想聽到—
That's enough! These people don't want to hear—

PETER: Kě tā men yīng gāi tīng. Tā men yīng gāi yào zhī dào—
可他們應該聽。他們應該要知道—
But they should. They should know—

This is not how people behave in China!

CAI: Nǐ huó xiàng gè wú zhī de lǎo wài nǐ zhī dào ma?
你活像個無知的老外你知道嗎？
You're acting like an ignorant foreigner!

PETER: Wǒ?
我？
Me?

Wǒ ài zhè ge guó jiā!
我愛這個國家！
I love this country!

Nǐ gēn wǒ zhēng qǔ de dōu yī yàng!

你跟我爭取的都一樣！

You and I are fighting for the same things!

Zài wǒ nèi xīn, wǒ shì zhōng guó rén!

在我內心，我是中國人！

In my heart, I am Chinese!

XI: Gòu le!

夠了！

Enough!

BING *(Cracking up)*: Qǐ yè jiè lǐ dōu shì fēng zi!

企業界裡都是瘋子！

The business world is crazy!

XI: Bǐ dé lǎo shī, ní biǎo dá guò nǐ de yì jiàn,

彼得老師，你表達過你的意見，

You've had your say, Teacher Peter.

Xiǎng shòu guò dǎng hé xiàn fǎ fù yǔ de yán lùn zì yóu,

享受過黨和憲法賦予的言論自由，

Enjoyed free speech under the Party's laws.

Jú zhǎng yào gǎn qù xià yí gè huì yì le.

局長要趕去下一個會議了。

The Minister is late for his next meeting.

(She cues Bing.)

BING: The Minister take me, going lunch.

PETER: Jú zhǎng, wǒ—duì bu qǐ.

局長，我—對不起。

Minister, I—I'm sorry.

Wǒ bù zhī dào zì jǐ zhè shì zěn me le—
我不知道自己這是怎麼了—
I don't know what came over—

(Cai leaves the room.)

XI: Sorry, Peter.

(Xi exits.)

BING: Rudeness is as rudeness does.

(Bing exits.)

PETER: The Minister and I are experiencing a misunderstanding, which
I fully intend to resolve.

(Peter exits, with Daniel following.)

Scene 8

*Daniel, in his hotel room. Xi enters, wearing dark glasses, an over-
coat, and a shawl around her hair.*

DANIEL: So what happened in there?
XI: Coat. Please.

(Daniel helps Xi remove her coat.)

DANIEL: Sorry. Seems I've forgotten my // manners.

XI: Zhēn dǎo méi. Yào zài zhè fáng jiān lǐ tán shēng yì.
真倒霉, 要在這房間裡談生意 。
Such a shame. To talk business in this room.

Problem. Unexpected discussion.

DANIEL: Cai said "no deal." Just like you told me he would.

XI: Yes.

DANIEL: So now, hooray?

XI: But. Teacher Peter—he acts, not in accordance.

DANIEL: Yeah, I didn't catch all of that, but // —wow!

XI: Problem. Credible is now doubt.

DANIEL: Credibility.

XI: Yes.

DANIEL: Of my company? In doubt?

XI: Yes. No. Yes.

DANIEL: Why? Cai has seen our website, right?

(He goes to his laptop.)

In anticipation of this contract, we just added a banner in Chinese.

XI: No, not website. Website is— *(Looking at the screen)* Chinese?

DANIEL: With our phone number. If anyone else over here wants to reach us, they can just dial headquarters in Cleveland directly and—

XI: Translation—very bad.

DANIEL: Really? We hired a grad student from Case Western who—

XI: 「Dǎ diàn huà wǒ men kuài jié zì yóu tóu dì」.

「打電話我們快捷自由投遞」。

"Call us for fast free delivery."

DANIEL: What does that mean?

XI: Never mind.

(She closes the laptop.)

Cannot have no credibility. With Peter.

DANIEL: Because he insulted // the Minister?

XI: Back door—all close. Therefore, you also must close.

DANIEL: I've got to get rid of Peter?

XI: Cut him.

DANIEL: If I do, will Cai change // his—?

XI: Forget Cai!

DANIEL: Peter. Is my problem?

XI: Yes.

DANIEL: Not Cai.

XI: Yes.

DANIEL: Cai is *not* my problem.

XI: Yes. Now, you understand.

DANIEL: I think . . .

XI: Good. So no more the business.

(She undoes his trousers, his pants fall to the floor.)

Look. *(She pulls a bottle from her purse)* Western luxury item. *(She hands it to Daniel)*

DANIEL: "Mr. Bubble."

XI: Yes?

DANIEL: Yeah, we use this all the time. I mean, mostly my kids, but . . .

XI *(Points to bathroom)*: So—go.

(Daniel exits to the bathroom. We hear bath water running off-stage. Xi starts to undress.

Then, going to the desk, Xi swipes her finger across the mousepad of Daniel's laptop. The computer comes to life.

She studies the Ohio Signage website.

She laughs:)

Kuài jié zì yóu tóu dì!

「 快捷自由投遞 」!

"Fast free delivery!"

Zhēn shǎ!

真傻！

This is so silly!

(To Daniel, offstage) Eh! Chinese person call Cleveland. You have someone answer, can speak Chinese?

DANIEL *(From offstage)*: Sorry, I can't hear you!

(On her cell phone, she dials the number from the website. A cell phone rings in their room.
    Daniel turns off the bath water. Entering the room, he picks up his pants from the floor. From his pant's pocket, he extracts his ringing cell phone.
    He sees Xi on her phone, notices his laptop awake.
    She ends her call. The ringing stops.)

It's a real company.

XI: I cannot—

DANIEL: It exists.

XI: Ringing to // your—?

DANIEL: It just doesn't . . . look like that.

XI *(Examining the website)*: China number, U.S. number—

DANIEL: Anymore.

XI: Same. Same! Where is company?

DANIEL: In Cleveland. // Like I—

XI: In your pant? Company in your pant?

DANIEL: Like I said! Family-run firm.

XI: "Hello? Pant? You make fast free delivery?"

DANIEL: Founded 1925. It's all true.

XI: Shit! Inside the pant. Shit!

DANIEL: Please. Let me // explain this!

XI: Company—shit!

DANIEL: Could you just calm // down?

XI: Hái yǐ wéi wǒ men shì yī huǒ de.
    還以為我們是一伙的 。
    I thought you were my partner.

(She starts to get dressed.)

DANIEL: Please. That's not helping.

XI: Wǒ mào duō dà fēng xiǎn a.
我冒多大風險啊。
I have taken major risks.

Risking for you!

DANIEL: Let's at least stay in the same language.

XI: Same language? Same?

DANIEL: Yeah because—

XI: Chinese! You speak Chinese!

DANIEL: Well, that's // a—

XI: You come here China, you speak Chinese!

DANIEL: It's a solution, but an impossible one!

XI: Xī fāng rén zǒng shì qī piàn wǒ men,
西方人總是欺騙我們,
Westerners have always fed us lies.

Suó yí wǒ xìn fèng ài guó zhǔ yì.
所以我信奉愛國主義。
That's why I'm a Chinese Nationalist.

DANIEL: I wish I *could* understand you, believe me—

XI: Wǒ men kuài yào dǎo guò lái lì yòng nǐ!
我們快要倒過來利用你!
But soon, it will be our turn to use you!

What come around, go around!

DANIEL: They say that? In Sri Lanka?

XI: One day, China will be strong!

(She grabs her overcoat.)

DANIEL: Wait. What are you—? "One day"? You're strong now! *We're*
the ones who are weak!

(Pause.)

XI: What?

DANIEL: China—strong! America—weak!

XI: Some day.

DANIEL: No. Now!

XI: Now? America weak?

DANIEL: And China strong!

(She starts to laugh.)

Is that a . . . funny laugh or an evil laugh?

XI: Zhè jiù shì wèi shén me yào chāo guò měi guó zǒng shì nà me kùn nán.

這就是為什麼要超過美國總是那麼困難。

This is why it's so difficult to get ahead of America.

DANIEL: Just—don't walk out on me, OK?

XI: Yīn wèi jiù shì qiáng dà de shí hòu,

因為就是強大的時候，

Even when you are strong,

nǐ men yé jiǎ zhuāng ruǎn ruò.

你們也假裝軟弱。

you still act like you're weak.

DANIEL: Can I . . . take your coat?

(She lets him take her coat.)

XI: Hǎo ba, fǎn zhèng wó yǐ jīng gòu zāo le.

好吧, 反正我已經夠糟了。

Why not? I'm already in deep shit.

Deal. Now disaster.

DANIEL: No, no—it doesn't have to be. We can. Do the job.

XI: "We"?

DANIEL: Ohio Signage. My great-grandfather founded it. True. But now, Cleveland. Economy, very bad.

XI: Yes.

DANIEL: Actually, it wasn't just the economy. It was stupid. Stupid. Business Decisions. Understand?

XI: Stupid.

DANIEL: They tried to go national. So . . . They ran. Company. Into the Ground. Stupid.

XI: Stupid. You?

DANIEL: No, no, not me. I didn't make those decisions.

XI: Then who?

DANIEL: My brother.

XI: Brother hold the bag.

DANIEL: He ran. The company. He made the stupid decisions.

XI: So today. Still stupid.

DANIEL: No, not today. Now, I run company. Brother gone.

XI: She gone.

DANIEL: He. Yes. So now, Ohio Signage is poised to—

XI: Secretary, he also gone? Worker, she also gone? *(Points to website)* Building, they also gone?

(Pause.)

DANIEL: For the moment, yes.

XI: So. You run company? You run—only you. *(She waves her cell phone)* Sorry. Daniel. This deal, cannot.

DANIEL: Why not? We can. Hire workers. Again.

XI: You—nobody!

(Pause.)

Your brother, she run company. Your silent, make run into ground?

DANIEL: Look, I wasn't there.

XI: This cannot sell.

DANIEL: Lemme make this—! I was. Not at the Company. During, during Stupid Decision Time!

XI: No? Then, where?

DANIEL: In Houston. Texas! Working in finance. Banking!

XI: Yuè shuō yuè bú duì jìn le.

越說越不對勁了。

This just gets worse.

DANIEL: But now I'm back. And I know. How to run a business. No more Stupid Decision Time!

XI: Company—already run in ground. Why you are not in the home? Why you permit such losing? Why you not return? Your brother, help her during Stupid Decision Time? Why she losing company? Why, you cannot preserve her?

DANIEL: Him! Him! My brother is a "him"! Christ, are you an idiot?

(Pause.)

I'm sorry, I didn't . . .

(She heads for the door.)

I'm broke. My family. No money. I'm so sorry. That I lied to you. But I can be better. If I can just get the deal. I can be that good man.

XI: American, like the children. Your business—picture only. You cannot even save the brother. Good-bye.

(She crosses to the door.)

DANIEL: You wanna know why couldn't I help my brother? Because I almost went to jail.

(Pause.)

Yeah. Jail. That's another little detail I forgot to mention. You ever hear of Enron?

XI: Enron.

DANIEL: Sure, everyone's heard of Enron. Even over here.

XI: Big—scandal?

DANIEL: Oh, yeah, the biggest. Well, it was back then. I wasn't one of the top dogs. Thank god. The prosecuters let me go. All I had to do was testify against my former bosses—my ex-friends. That's why I couldn't go to Cleveland and save the company! Because I was busy saving my own ass!

XI: Enron—you?

DANIEL: Enron me. Wanna see?

(He pulls up a website on his laptop.)

There I am. In the fucking *Houston Chronicle*. I wore better suits back then. But you can still see me. In the back.

XI: That, you.

DANIEL: Yup. This would've gone over big, huh? If we'd tried to convince the Chinese government to get into bed with an ex-Enron guy? No one at home will touch me! But I thought—maybe if I went all the way to China, steered clear of the big cities— maybe I could pull this off. Take the ruined shell of my family firm. Land a deal. And become someone new. Someplace far away, where hardly anyone can understand a word I'm saying.

(Pause.)

If it'd gone another way . . . I could've loved you.

XI: You. Good man, honest man.

DANIEL: What?

XI: Now, is possible.

(The lights fade to black.)

Act Two

————

Scene 9

The lobby of Daniel's hotel. Peter paces. He's on his cell phone.

PETER *(Into his phone)*: Daniel. It's Peter. I'm down in your lobby. This is my third message. Listen, I still think we can salvage this. Cai's position in the Party is very weak. The Party Secretary feels he's been too slow to implement market reforms. They're looking for any excuse to sack him. Which presents us with . . .

(The elevator door opens. Xi and Daniel exit together.)

Fù jú zhǎng?
副局長？
Vice Minister?

DANIEL: Oh.

(Stepping back, Peter takes in Xi and Daniel.)

PETER: Every now and then, a mystery becomes clear.

Nǐ men duō jiǔ le?

你們多久了？

How long has this been going on?

XI *(To Daniel)*: He is making the conclusion.

DANIEL: Peter, look, it's over between us.

PETER: You couldn't have let me know? About the two of you?

DANIEL: You don't know what you're talking about. Just go.

(Daniel starts to walk away, then:)

PETER: I'm your consultant! What happened to all your talk? About "honesty." "If we're not open, who can be?"

DANIEL: Oh, get off it! Lecturing *me* about "honesty"? Mr. "Consultant"? Maybe on, on ancient Ming porcelains or, or dipsy-shit calligraphy. But you don't know the first thing about business.

(Pause.)

Believe it or not, back in the States, we also have to please our bosses! And you know what that requires? Self-control. You don't always say what's on your mind. You don't blurt out to someone who can make or break you—you don't tell him what he's doing is stupid. Or illegal. You just go along—with everything you've got!

(Pause.)

And in China? Hell, I don't need a "consultant" who, in the middle of the Big Meeting, suddenly suffers a nervous breakdown and starts screaming that my client's only son is a fucking moron!

PETER: I had better bloody well receive my commission. In fact, I think you owe me a substantial bonus. For keeping my mouth shut.

DANIEL: I don't care who you fucking tell.

PETER *(To Xi)*: Nǐ zài hu de shì ba?
你在乎的是吧？
You care, don't you?

Rú guó wǒ gào su qí tā rén?
如果我告訴其他人？
If I tell people?

XI: Gào sù tā men shén me ne?
告訴他們什麼呢？
Tell them what?

PETER: Guān yú nǐ gēn tā . . .
關於你跟他……
That you and he are . . .

XI: Shén me?
什麼？
Yes?

PETER: Gǎo shàng le!
搞上了！
Carrying on an affair!

XI: Ní zěn me ké yǐ xià zhè yàng de jié lùn?
你怎麼可以下這樣的結論？
How can you draw such a conclusion?

Cài jú zhǎng pài wǒ lái jiàn kǎ fán nuò xiān sheng, nǐ shì zhī
dào de.
蔡局長派我來見卡凡諾先生, 你是知道的 。
You know Minister Cai has sent me to meet Mr. Cavanaugh.

Zhè jiù shì nǐ shī bài de yuán yīn.

這就是你失敗的原因—

This is why you failed to become a consultant.

Yīn wèi nǐ zhè ge gù wèn de guān diǎn, yī diǎn dōu bù kě kào.

因為你這個顧問的觀點, 一點都不可靠 。

Because your perceptions are not so credible.

PETER: Nà nǐ de zhàng fū huì zěn me xiǎng?

那你的丈夫會怎麼想 ？

And what would your husband think?

XI: Nǐ yào xiǎng zhī dào wǒ gào sù nǐ ba,

你要想知道我告訴你吧,

If you must know,

wó suǒ zuò de shì wó lǎo gōng quán dōu zhī dào,

我所做的事我老公全都知道,

my husband is aware of all my business.

Ér qiě tā yī diǎn yì jiàn yě méi yǒu.

而且他一點意見也沒有 。

And he's fine with everything.

Wait here for car, Mr. Cavanaugh.

(Pause.)

PETER: No! No—

Bié xiǎng yī zóu liǎo zhī!

別想一走了之 ！

You are not going to get away with this!

XI: Bǐ dé lǎo shī, wǒ men zhī jiān méi yǒu shén me bù kě gào rén de shì.

彼得老師, 我們之間沒有什麼不可告人的事 。

We have no secrets, Teacher Peter.

(A Hotel Manager enters, drawn by the commotion of Peter's rant.)

PETER: Nà shì huǎng yán!

那是謊言！

That's a lie!

Jiù xiàng zhè guó jiā lǐ miàn de suó yóu huǎng yán!

就像這國家裡面的所有謊言！

Like all the other lies in this country!

(Pause.)

"Do my son this favor, and you can have whatever you want."

(He continues:)

Shén me yǒu zhōng guó tè sè de shè huì zhǔ yì, nà suàn shén me?

什麼有中國特色的社會主義, 那算什麼？

"Socialism with Chinese characteristics." What does that even mean?

Hái yǒu nà ge zuì dà de huǎng yán!

還有那個最大的謊言！

And here is the biggest lie of all!

Zhōng guó shì shè huì zhǔ yì guó jiā, dǎng shì wèi rén mín fú wù?

中國是社會主義國家, 黨是為人民服務？

China is a socialist state, run for the benefit of the people?

Quán shì gǒu pì!

全是狗屁！

What a load of crap!

Nà xiē gàn bù dōu shì zuì fàn, yīng gāi bǎ tā men quán dōu lā
qù zuò láo!
那些幹部都是罪犯, 應該把他們全都拉去坐牢！
Party officials are criminals, who should all be in jail!

XI: Bǐ dé lǎo shī! Bú yào zài shuō le!
彼得老師！不要再說了！
Teacher Peter! Stop now!

*(Xi, Peter and Daniel see the Hotel Manager, who snaps a photo
of Peter on her cell phone, then exits.)*

Shī péi le.
失陪了。
I'm very sorry.

(Xi exits.)

DANIEL: I'm not sure what just happened there, but I don't think it
went well for you.
PETER: She was just a hotel manager, she's not going to tell anyone.
DANIEL: What *did* you say?
PETER: I wasn't too loud, was I?
DANIEL: What did you // say?
PETER: Stupid! What is wrong with me? There's a certain tolerance
here for unhinged foreigners, but will anybody hire one? I should
never have tried to do this.
DANIEL: Do what?
PETER: Pass myself off as a—a consultant. Which I'm not. I'm sorry.
DANIEL: We all do what we have to.
PETER: That's exactly it! Back in the old days, a Westerner who could
speak Chinese like a native—employers fought to give me jobs.
And the women? I could walk down any street—they'd point
and giggle—whispering how tall I was.
DANIEL: Really? 'Cause I gotta say, the people here aren't as short //
as I—

PETER: I know, I'm not so tall any longer! But back then, I was.

(Pause.)

Today, in the major cities—foreigners are everywhere. Speaking good Chinese. But they're architects and accountants and financial analysts and . . .

DANIEL: Did you ever think maybe . . . it's time for you to go home?

PETER: England? I've tried that, too. For a year, back in Leicester. But—no. Beyond learning to get by without someone to do my cooking, cleaning, washing—I felt this overwhelming sense of loss. I'd try explaining to people about all I'd learned over here. But they'd just look at me with these blank stares—as if I was speaking another language.

(A Driver enters.)

DRIVER: Car?

(He hands Daniel his card, then exits.)

DANIEL: Peter, I wish you well.

(They shake hands.)

Look, I know how it feels to twist yourself into a pretzel just 'cause you wanna make a deal. But lately, I've started thinking: Maybe I can just be myself. Be honest.

PETER: You've started thinking that—in China?

DANIEL: Yeah. Crazy huh?

(Daniel exits.)

Scene 10

A conference room. Seated at one table are Judge Geming, male,
forty to fifty, and Prosecutor Li, female, thirties.
   Xi sits across from them at another table, beside Daniel, who is
standing, addressing the group. His remarks are interpreted by a new
translator, Zhao, female.

DANIEL: We are a family-run firm, started in 1925.

ZHAO: Tā de gōng sī zài yī jiǔ èr wǔ nián chéng lì,
    他的公司在1925年成立,
    His company began in 1925.

    Ér tā de jiā rén xǐ huān yī qí pǎo bù.
    而他的家人喜歡一起跑步。
    And his family enjoys running together.

XI: Kǎ fán nuò xiān sheng lái zì kè lǐ fū lán,
    卡凡諾先生來自克里夫蘭,
    Mr. Cavanaugh is from Cleveland.

    Shì zài měi guó zhōng xī bù de yí gè chéng shì,
    是在美國中西部的一個城市,
    A city in America's "Midwest."

    Bú tài zhù míng, bú xiàng niǔ yuē huò zhě luò shān jī.
    不太著名, 不像紐約或者洛杉磯。
    Not famous, like New York or Los Angeles.

GEMING: Wǒ men guì yáng yě bú shì shén me yǒu míng de chéng shì,
    我們貴陽也不是什麼有名的城市,
    Here in Guiyang, we are also not famous.

Bú xiàng zhù míng de běi jīng huò shàng hǎi.

不像著名的北京或上海。

Not like the elites of Beijing or Shanghai.

ZHAO: Here in Guiyang, we despise the coastal elites.

DANIEL: You're Midwesterners!

XI: Tā shuō wǒ men quán shì nèi dì rén.

他說我們全是「內地人」。

He says, we are all "Midwesterners."

(They laugh.)

ZHAO: They laugh.

XI: É hài é zhōu zhāo pái shè jì gōng sī céng jīng hěn chū sè,

俄亥俄州招牌設計公司曾經很出色,

Ohio Signage was once a great company,

dàn bú xìng zài měi guó zuì jìn de jīng jì zāi nàn zhōng chéng wéi shòu hài zhě.

但不幸在美國最近的經濟災難中成為受害者。

which has recently fallen victim to America's economic disaster.

GEMING: Shì de, duì yú guì guó de jù é zhài wù, wǒ men fēi cháng tóng qíng.

是的, 對於貴國的巨額債務, 我們非常同情。

Yes, we sympathize with your massive debt.

ZHAO: The Magistrate knows all about the recent collapse of America.

LI: Kě zhè gēn tā men shì fóu yǒu zī gé wèi wén huà zhōng xīn zuò zhǐ shì pái yǒu shén me guān xi?

可這跟他們是否有資格為文化中心做指示牌有什麼關係？

But why should this qualify them to make signs for the Cultural Center?

ZHAO: Mrs. Li questions your company's qualifications.

(Li's cell phone rings. She answers it.)

LI: Bù, páng xiè!
不, 螃蟹！
No, crab!

Wǒ shuō wǒ yào páng xiè!
我說我要螃蟹！
I said, I want crab!

Bú shì! Shì páng xiè!
不是！是螃蟹！
No! Crab!

(She hangs up. To Daniel:)

Jì xù ba.
繼續吧。
Go on.

ZHAO: Keep going.
DANIEL: I recently assumed control of Ohio Signage and now direct all its operations.

ZHAO: Xiàn zài é hài é zhōu zhāo pái shè jì gōng sī yóu kǎ fán nuò xiān sheng kòng zhì—
現在俄亥俄州招牌設計公司由卡凡諾先生控制—
Mr. Cavanaugh now controls Ohio Signage and—

I am sorry. "Direct"—what?
DANIEL: All our operations.
ZHAO: Ah, thank you.

(To the group:)

Ér tā yě shì gè wài kē yī shēng.

而他也是個外科醫生。

And he is also a surgeon.

XI: Bù, bù! Kǎ fán nuò xiān sheng bú shì yī shēng!

不, 不！卡凡諾先生不是醫生！

No, no! Mr. Cavanaugh is not a doctor!

ZHAO: Duì bu qǐ.

對不起。

Apologies.

XI: Tā shì gè bèi shòu jìng zhòng de shāng rén,

他是個備受敬重的商人,

He is a respected businessman,

Xiàn zài gōng sī yóu tā guán lǐ.

現在公司由他管理。

now running the firm.

LI: Wǒ men wèi shén me yào xiāng xìn tā?

我們為什麼要相信他？

Why should we put our faith in him?

ZHAO: She doubts your personal integrity.

XI *(To Daniel)*: <Go on.> Honest man.

DANIEL: I came to Ohio Signage after six years working in senior management . . . at a company called Enron.

ZHAO: Really?

XI: Fān yì yā!

翻譯呀！

Just translate!

ZHAO: Kǎ fán nuò xiān sheng céng jīng zài ān rán dān rèn gāo jí xíng zhèng!
卡凡諾先生曾經在安然擔任高級行政！
Mr. Cavanaugh used to be an executive at Enron!

LI: Zhēn de? Ān rán?
真的？安然？
Really? Enron?

GEMING: Shì wǒ men bào shàng kàn de nà ge ān rán ma?
是我們報上看的那個安然嗎？
The same Enron we read about in the papers?

XI: Shì! Yuán lái tā shì cè huà nà zōng shì jiè chǒu wén de shóu nǎo zhī yī!
是！原來他是策劃那宗世界醜聞的首腦之一！
Yes! He is among the masterminds of that world-famous scandal!

(Li's phone rings. She answers it.)

LI *(Into phone)*: Bié shuō le! Wǒ zài máng ne!
別說了！我在忙呢！
Shut up! I'm busy!

(She hangs up.)

Tā shì guān jiàn rén wù ma? Wèn tā!
他是關鍵人物嗎？問他！
Was he a major player? Ask him!

ZHAO: Were you a small fish or a big pond?
DANIEL: Well, I was a salesman—I sold securities.

ZHAO: Tā de gōng zuò, jiù shì fàn mài ān quán de jiǎ xiàng.
他的工作，就是販賣安全的假象。
He sold customers the belief that they were secure.

XI: Tā shì gāo jí yíng yè yuán! Fù zé yī bǎi yī shí gè yì měi yuán de
zhèng quàn.

他是高級營業員！負責一百一十個億美元的證券 。

**He was a top salesman! Responsible for eleven billion dollars
of stock.**

ZHAO: She says you sold eleven billion U.S. dollar stock.
DANIEL: Not personally, // I was really—
LI: Kenneth Lay?

(Pause.)

Nǐ rèn shi kěn ní sī léi?

你認識肯尼斯雷？

Did you know Kenneth Lay?

DANIEL: Ken?
ZHAO: No! Kenneth. Lay. Do you know—?
DANIEL: Why, sure, I knew Kenneth. We stopped talking // when it
all fell apart, but . . .

ZHAO: Duì! Duì! Tā rèn shi kěn ní sī léi!

對！對！他認識肯尼斯雷！

Yes! Yes! He knows Kenneth Lay!

XI: Tā men yǐ qián shì hǎo péng yǒu!

他們以前是好朋友！

They were good friends!

LI: Nà me jié fū—

那麼傑夫 —

How about Jeffrey—

Tā xìng shén me lái zhe?

他姓什麼來著？

What is his first name?

LI, GEMING AND ZHAO: Jié fū—Jié fū—
傑夫—傑夫—
Jeffrey—Jeffrey—

DANIEL: Jeffrey Skilling? Are you // talking about—?

LI: Duì! Shǐ jì líng! Nǐ rèn shi tā ma?
對！史紀齡！你認識他嗎？
Yes! Jeffrey Skilling! Do you know him?

ZHAO: Do you know Mr. Skilling Jeffrey?
DANIEL: Yes, I knew Jeffrey, I knew all of them.

ZHAO: Tā quán bù dōu rèn shi!
他全部都認識！
He knows all of them!

GEMING: Ān dé lǔ fú sī tuō.
安德魯福斯托。
Andrew Fastow.

Jì dé tā ma?
記得他嗎？
Remember him?

Ō, tā kě huài ne.
噢, 他可壞呢。
Oh, he was a naughty one.

ZHAO: You know naughty Andrew?
DANIEL: Fastow? Maybe the smartest guy I ever met. Very guarded.
He could've been Chinese!

ZHAO: Tā shuō ān dé lǔ xiān sheng xiàng zhōng guó rén yí yàng cōng
míng!
他說安德魯先生像中國人一樣聰明！
He says Mr. Andrew was as smart as a Chinese!

LI, GEMING AND ZHAO: Ō bù bù bù bù bù . . .
噢不不不不不……
Oh no, no, no, no, no . . .

ZHAO: We are not so smart as Enron.

GEMING: Cān yù de rén qí zhōng yǒu yí gè zhōng guó rén, bú shì ma?
參與的人其中有一個中國人，不是嗎？
There was a Chinese guy involved, wasn't there?

LI: Duì! Lái zì nán jīng! Nà ge bái—shén me ne—
對！來自南京！那個白—什麼呢—
Yes! From Nanjing! Bai—somebody—

ZHAO: Wǒ sān yí shuō tā rèn shi nà ge rén de wú biǎo gē.
我三姨說她認識那個人的五表哥。
My third aunt knows his fifth cousin.

Nà ge bái lóu lóng.
那個白樓隆。
Bai Lou Long.

DANIEL: You're talking about Lou Lung Pai? Lou?

GEMING: Tā zhēn qǔ le gè tiào tuō yī wǔ de?
他真娶了個跳脫衣舞的？
Did he really marry the stripper?

(To Zhao:)

Wèn tā yā!
問他呀！
Ask him!

ZHAO: Did Mr. Bai wed the naked fun-time girl?
DANIEL: Melanie? Yeah, that's all true.

ZHAO: Shì de, shì zhēn de.

是的, 是真的 。

Yes, it's true.

DANIEL: That was quite a time . . .

XI: Kǎ fán nuò xiān sheng quán dōu zhī dào!

卡凡諾先生全都知道 !

Mr. Cavanaugh knew them all!

Tā guǒ rán shì nà chǎng zāi nàn de zhǔ yào cè huà rén!

他果然是那場災難的主要策劃人 !

He was a chief architect of the disaster!

ZHAO: She says you made possible the entire scandal!

DANIEL: No, I didn't—

ZHAO: Tā hěn qiān xū.

他很謙虛 。

He is modest.

DANIEL: OK, maybe I did.

ZHAO: Tā chéng rèn le.

他承認了 。

He agrees.

XI: Yī bǎi yī shí gè yì měi yuán!

一百一十個億美元 !

Eleven billion dollars!

Nà shì měi guó yǒu shí yǐ lái zuì yán zhòng de jīn róng zāi nàn!

那是美國有史以來最嚴重的金融災難 !

The biggest financial collapse in American history!

LI: Hòu lái lù xù yǒu gèng duō gèng yán zhòng de jīng jì wēi jī.

後來陸續有更多更嚴重的經濟危機。

There have been many larger ones since.

ZHAO: She says your disaster, now, not so impressive.

DANIEL: But we were the first!

ZHAO: Ān rán kě shì dì yī gè!

安然可是第一個！

Enron was first!

LI: Méi cuò, méi cuò.

沒錯、沒錯。

True, true.

ZHAO: She agrees.

GEMING: Wǒ kàn, xiàn zài shì qíng qīng chú le.

我看，現在事情清楚了。

Well, I think the situation now is clear.

Wǒ men cóng lái méi yǒu zhè me yī wèi guó jì zhī míng de jīn róng rén wù

我們從來沒有這麼一位國際知名的金融人物

Never has such a world-famous financial figure

dào wǒ men guì yáng lái zuò shēng yì.

到我們貴陽來做生意。

come to Guiyang to do business.

ZHAO: The Magistrate appreciates your high status.

DANIEL: Oh no, no, no, no, no, no. I'm just an ordinary American businessman—hoping to bring high-quality signage to your great city.

ZHAO: Tā kè qì dì qǐng qiú wéi guì yáng zuò zhǐ shì pái.

他客氣地請求為貴陽做指示牌。

He humbly seeks to make signs for Guiyang.

LI: Cài jú zhǎng jìng rán jù jué zhè xiàng hé zuò,
蔡局長竟然拒絕這項合作,
For Minister Cai to have rejected such an offer

yí dìng yǒu wèn tí.
一定有問題 。
certainly warrants an investigation.

ZHAO: The Prosecuter says Cai now swims in the hot water.

(Geming stands.)

GEMING: Gǎn xiè nǐ jīn tiān lái gēn wǒ men jiàn miàn.
感謝你今天來跟我們見面 。
Thank you for coming to talk with us today.

ZHAO: Thank you.
DANIEL: No, thank you.

ZHAO: Xiè xie.
謝謝 。
Thank you.

LI *(To Daniel)*: Xiè xie.
謝謝 。
Thank you.

ZHAO: Thank you.
DANIEL *(To Li)*: No, thank you.

ZHAO: Xiè xie.
謝謝 。
Thank you.

(Daniel starts to go, then:)

GEMING: Zhè jiù shì zhēn zhèng de jīn róng cái jùn.

這就是真正的金融才俊 。

There goes a true high-roller.

ZHAO: You roll the big craps.

DANIEL: The—? Oh! You mean, like in gambling?

ZHAO: Yes. The big craps.

DANIEL: So I'm a—high-roller? Well, isn't that what business is all about?

ZHAO: Tā zài gài niàn shàng tóng yì nín de shuō fǎ.

他在概念上同意您的說法 。

He is in ideological agreement.

XI: Wǒ lái sòng kǎ fán nuò xiān sheng.

我來送卡凡諾先生 。

I will show Mr. Cavanaugh to the door.

(Daniel and Xi exit.)

GEMING: Wǒ huì qǐng nà ge wài guó rén chī dùn fàn.

我會請那個外國人吃頓飯 。

I'm going to invite that foreigner to dinner.

LI: Wó yě qù ba!

我也去吧 !

I'll come, too!

Āi, ní xiǎng tā huì bu huì rèn shi léi màn xiōng dì de rén?

哎, 你想他會不會認識雷曼兄弟的人 ?

Hey, you think he knows any of the Lehman Brothers?

Scene 11

Tight spot on Xi, in bed.

XI: Zuò diàn tī shàng tā fáng jiān de shí hòu,
坐電梯上他房間的時候,
On the way up to his room,

wǒ biàn chéng lìng yí gè nǚ rén.
我變成另一個女人 。
I become another woman.

Yí gè duì zhàng fu bù zhōng de nǚ rén,
一個對丈夫不忠的女人,
One who cheats on her husband,

ér qiě, tā hái shì gè wài guó rén.
而且, 他還是個外國人 。
with a foreigner, even worse.

Wǒ men shì xīn shēng dài,
我們是新生代,
We were the new generation,

huì tiāo zì jǐ de hǎo nán rén, suí xīn suǒ ài.
會挑自己的好男人, 隨心所愛 。
who would pick good men, and live for love.

Wǒ shén me dōu zuò duì le,
我什麼都做對了,
I did everything right.

Dàn shì xiàn zài, wǒ huì bǐ tī zhe sān cùn jīn lián, máng hūn yǎ jià de lǎo lao
但是現在, 我會比踢著三吋金蓮 、盲婚啞嫁的姥姥
Yet now, am I any happier than my grandmother

huó de gèng kuài lè ma?

活得更快樂嗎？

with her arranged marriage and bound feet?

(Lights up on Daniel's hotel room.)

DANIEL: Tell me again. Just because clarity is— They Will. Give me
   the Deal. Yes?
XI: Yes.
DANIEL: God, this is so—I could just—I think I will.

(He kisses her.)

Let's go out. Celebrate.
XI: Cannot moving without the clothes.

(Pause.)

DANIEL: You're absolutely right, let's stay in.

(They fall onto the bed. As they undress one another:)

It's starting to happen, you know.

XI: Zhè zhèng shì wǒ xiàn zài xū yào de.

這正是我現在需要的。

This is exactly what I need right now.

DANIEL: That thing I said before.

XI: Wàng diào yí qiè.

忘掉一切。

To forget everything.

DANIEL: Whatever you're saying, I agree.
XI: Agree.

DANIEL: Agree!
XI: Is better this way.
DANIEL: Agree, agree!

(As he slowly kisses down her body:)

It's so—I've just   XI: Qù wàng jì shēng huó zhòng dì yī qiè . . .
never felt like   去忘記生活中的一切……
this before. And   **To forget everything in my life . . .**
so that thing—
when I said,   fàng xia sī xiǎng, ràng shēn tǐ jìn rù
"I could've   wàng wǒ de zhuàng tài . . .
loved you"?—I   放下思想, 讓身體進入忘我的狀
think I was right.   態……
I think, it's   **leave my mind and let my body take**
happening.   **me away . . .**

gǎn jué xià tǐ jiàn jiàn shī rùn . . .
感覺下體漸漸濕潤……
feel myself getting wetter . . .

zhěng gè shì jiè dōu zài qī dài . . .
整個世界都在期待……
as all the world becomes anticipation . . .

(In the clear:)

ràng wǒ jìn qíng dì ài.
讓我盡情地愛 。
and I can just be in love.

(Daniel looks up from her body.)

DANIEL: You, too?
XI: What?
DANIEL: "Ai." You said "ai," didn't you?

XI: Zài wǎng xià diǎn!
再往下點！
Lower!

Ní xiǎng shuō shén me dōu xíng, dàn bú yào tíng xià lái.
你想說什麼都行，但不要停下來。
Say whatever you want, but don't stop.

(He resumes caressing her.)

DANIEL: Ai.
XI *(Warmly)*: Yes, you . . .
DANIEL: No, not me. "Ai."

XI: Bié sǎo xìng, bài tuō, bié pò huài qì fēn.
別掃興，拜託，別破壞氣氛。
Don't ruin this, please don't ruin this.

DANIEL: "Ai." It means "love," doesn't it?
XI: Hah? Oh!

(Pause.)

Ài.
愛。
Love.

DANIEL: Yes!

(Pause.)

Āi.
埃。
Dust.

XI: No.

(Pause.)

Ài.
愛。
Love.

DANIEL: Ài.
愛。
Love.

(Pause.)

It sounds . . . right. Can you teach me, one more thing?

(Pause.)

Yes?

XI: "Shi."

DANIEL: Sure. I want to say—

XI: No. "Shi." Chinese: "yes" is "shi."

DANIEL: Huh? Wait. No.

XI: "No." "Bu shi."

DANIEL: Hold on. I meant. I want to say, "I love you."

(Pause.)

XI: Wǒ ài nǐ.
我愛你。
I love you.

DANIEL: Wǔ ā yí.
五阿姨。
My fifth aunt.

Is that right?

(Pause.)

XI: Yes. Right.

DANIEL: Really? No corrections? Tonal? That would be a first.

(Pause.)

Wú wèi le.
無謂了 。
Absolutely useless.

(Pause.)

There I was, thinking I had to lie about my past. Cover it up. But you knew, I could tell the truth. And everything would be OK. Better than OK. That by telling the truth. I got the deal. Got my Guanxi.

(Pause.)

All the time, it was always you.

(Pause.)

Wū hǎi ní.
污海泥 。
Dirty sea mud.

(She laughs.)

Wō ài niú.
蝸愛牛 。
Snail loves cow.

Wā ài niào.
蛙愛尿 。
Frog loves to pee.

I'm gonna get it right. 'Cause I only tell the truth now. And I will.
Even to my wife.

(She stops laughing.)

XI: "Wife"?
DANIEL: Oh, that got your attention.
XI: What saying, your "wife"?
DANIEL: Down in the lobby? When Peter "caught" us? Suddenly, it
hit me. I want to tell. I want the whole world to know!

(Pause.)

And I'll start. By telling my wife.
XI: Telling your wife the fucking?
DANIEL: Wow, I didn't even know you knew // that word.
XI: No!
DANIEL: Not the—telling my wife. —That I'm in love with you.
XI: Such thing, you cannot.
DANIEL: Why // not?
XI: Your wife, wife!
DANIEL: Um, yeah, but I love you!
XI: Is not important.
DANIEL: Not // important?
XI: Telling truth to wife? For why?
DANIEL: Because I'm an honest man. Right?
XI: Yes.
DANIEL: Good man.
XI: Yes.
DANIEL: And good, honest men—tell their wives the truth.
XI: No.
DANIEL: No?
XI: Good honest man, respecting the wife.
DANIEL: I respect my wife—
XI: Yes.
DANIEL: —by lying to her?

XI: Of course!

(Pause.)

DANIEL: Is that what you do? You? Respect your husband?
XI: Yes.
DANIEL: By having sex with me?
XI: And do not tell.
DANIEL: You said you wanted to escape your marriage.
XI: Yes. Escaping—with you.
DANIEL: That's what I want, too! But—it's hard—"not so easy"—to end it in China?
XI: Hah?
DANIEL: Hard? To end marriage? In China?
XI: No. Easy.
DANIEL: But you said—
XI: End marriage, easy. Escape, hard.
DANIEL: I don't—
XI: The long marriage. Like work, work, work. Then escape. No escape, only working is, um, death. Marriage, same. Also, death. Unless, escape.

(Pause.)

But, not so easy. In Guiyang, so much people, they know me.
DANIEL: I am—your escape?
XI: Mmmm.
DANIEL: That's all?
XI: So much escape.
DANIEL: I'm like—what, a "vacation"? From your "real job"?
XI: From the death.
DANIEL: No, no, no. You told me you don't love your husband.
XI: Husband? No!
DANIEL: Well, I love you. And I think—you love me.
XI: Yes. Very nice.

DANIEL: It's more than just "nice," it's—it's what we're meant to do. Find the person we love. And be together. For the rest of our lives. *(Grabs her by the shoulders)* I believe "ai" can last a lifetime.

XI: Jesus Christ.

DANIEL: I'm sorry?

XI: Also, Jesus Christ, you are believing?

(She kisses him.)

「Ài」, jiù shì nǐ men měi guó rén de zōng jiào.
「愛」, 就是你們美國人的宗教 。
"Love," it is your American religion.

(He pulls away.)

DANIEL: So it doesn't matter to you? You want to stay married. Even though, you and your husband—no "ai"?

XI: No. "Qíng yì."

DANIEL: Qíng—what?

XI: Qíng yì. Marriage: Qíng yì.

DANIEL: And what does that mean?

XI: Qíng yì is like comrade.

DANIEL: Comrade. Like Chairman Mao?

XI: Ah, no. I cannot know him. No, again. Is like the "righteous."

DANIEL: So marriage—is an act of "righteousness"?

XI: No, no, no. Ah, very subtle. *(Pause)* "Committing"!

DANIEL: Commitment. Like a commitment to a contract?

XI: No, no, no. More feeling!

DANIEL: I don't think there's a word in English.

(Pause.)

Look, you believe. Your marriage. Is like a trap. Trap, you understand?

Xi uses the Chinese term, "Qíng yì," 情義, for which there is no direct English translation.

XI: Marriage, trap. Yes, same.

DANIEL: But It Doesn't Have To Be That Way. Marriage. Can Be More.

XI: More?

DANIEL: Yes!

(He looks into her eyes.)

Very rare. Two people, find each other. Deep. From this. We build.
A life together. A new life. A good life. Now, you understand?

(She pulls away from him.)

XI: Nǐ wèi shén me yào zhè yàng zuò?
    你為什麼要這樣做？
    Why are you doing this?

(Pause.)

Ruin everything!

DANIEL: You helped me.

XI: I help you. Yes.

DANIEL: Wasn't it because you saw a good man?

(Pause.)

Why did you help me? Why?

XI: For Cai back door!

DANIEL: Not this again . . .

XI: You wanting truth?! You wanting honest?! Helping you, to remove
    Cai from the Minister.

DANIEL: You wanted . . . to get rid of Cai?

XI: Market reform, slow, slow. Yet Cai, protection by Mayor, cannot
    remove. But now, Cai wife sister—

DANIEL: Cai's sister-in-law—

XI: —against the Enron? Yet, still Cai say no? Corruption! Therefore,
    removal.

DANIEL: You did all this to take down Cai? Why? Do you hate him? Or, so you can be Minister?

XI: I? Minister? No!

DANIEL: Well, then—

XI: Too much pressuring.

DANIEL: Then, what is it? Cai removal. Help who?

(Pause.)

Help who?

XI: Help the Judge.

DANIEL: Who's the Judge?

XI: Judge. You see him! In courthouse!

DANIEL: The conference room? Where we had our meeting today?

XI: Yes!

DANIEL: Are you talking about the Magistrate?

XI: "Magistrate"? Translation, very bad.

(Pause.)

He is Judge. By removal Cai, Party Secretary, very happy. Market reform, now go fast! Therefore Judge—he gains the Guanxi.

DANIEL: So that Judge, he'll be in for some kind of—promotion?

XI: Yes! Promotion!

DANIEL: But I still don't—why would you—? Who is he? Why would you go to all this trouble to help that? . . .

(Pause.)

The Judge—he's your husband.

XI: Yes.

DANIEL: You did all this—to help your husband?

XI: Yes.

DANIEL: Including—having sex with me?

(Pause.)

XI: No.

(Pause.)

Wǒ wéi zì jǐ zhuī qiú luó màn dì kè,
我為自己追求羅曼蒂克,
The romance was for me.

Bú wèi bié rén.
不為別人 。
Just me.

DANIEL: English?

XI: I, perfection. Cannot. Try, but cannot. So hard the attempting, yet still—home, family, silence—the death never ending. And so, therefore, cannot. Yet good, enough good, to be wife, can.

(Pause. She fights back tears.)

DANIEL: That word—from before—

XI: Qíng yì.

DANIEL: Qíng yì.

XI: Now you understand.

(She starts to dress.)

DANIEL: Wait. But does that mean you have to—?

XI: Good-bye.

DANIEL: But why? We can still . . . Why?

XI: Face change.

(Pause.)

Nǐ bù zūn zhòng nǐ de hūn yīn,
你不尊重你的婚姻,
If you do not respect your marriage,

yě huì wēi xié dào wǒ de hūn yīn.
也會威脅到我的婚姻。
then you are a threat to mine.

(Pause.)

Such sleepy.

(She finishes gathering her things, heads for the door.)

DANIEL: But now I can be that good man.
XI: Before, escape. Now, I am sleeping with you.

(She exits.)

Scene 12

Cai's home. Cai, half dressed, in khaki green pants and undershirt, escorts Peter into his living room.

PETER: Qù guò nǐ bàn gōng shì, tā men shuō nǐ zài jiā lǐ.
去過你辦公室, 他們說你在家裡。
Your office told me you were at home.

CAI: Zǎo shàng shì zhǎng bàn gōng shì lí yǒu péng yóu géi wó dǎ diàn huà,
早上市長辦公室裡有朋友給我打電話,
A friend from the Mayor's office called this morning.

Jiàn yì wǒ jīn tiān bú yào shàng bān.
建議我今天不要上班。
Said it'd be better if I didn't go in to work today.

PETER: Yuán lái shì zhè yang.
原來是這樣。
I see.

CAI: Gōng ān dào dá yǐ qián nǐ kuài lí kāi ba,
公安到達以前你快離開吧,
You don't want to be here when the police arrive.

Bèi fā xiàn gēn wó yǒu lián xì bù hǎo,
被發現跟我有聯繫不好,
It will be bad for you to be associated

wǒ shì yí gè 「tān wū guān yuán」.
我是一個「 貪污官員 」。
with a "corrupt official."

Shù wǒ bù néng zhāo dài nǐ,
恕我不能招待你,
Forgive my poor hospitality.

Dài huì bèi dài zǒu, ràng wó bǎo liú yī diǎn zūn yán.
待會被帶走, 讓我保留一點尊嚴 。
I just want to leave home with some pride.

(He resumes dressing himself.)

PETER: Wǒ lái xiàng nǐ dào qiàn de.
我來向你道歉的 。
I came to ask your forgiveness.

Wǒ méi xiǎng dào dài nà ge měi guó rén qù jiàn nǐ,
我沒想到帶那個美國人去見你,
When I brought the American to you,

huì bá nǐ lián lèi chéng zhè yàng zǐ.
會把你連累成這樣子 。
I never dreamed it would lead to this.

CAI: Qí mǎ qù le láo fáng,
起碼去了牢房,
At least in prison,

wǒ jiù bú yòng tīng dào wó lǎo pó de shēng yīn le.
我就不用聽到我老婆的聲音了 。
I will no longer have to listen to my wife.

Nà nǐ ne?
那你呢 ？
And you?

Nǐ huí qù jiāo shū le ma?
你回去教書了嗎 ？
You've gone back to teaching?

PETER: Shì de, suī rán huà chuán kāi le, shuō wǒ xíng wéi bù lǐ xìng,
是的, 雖然話傳開了, 說我行為不理性,
Yes, word got around that I was acting irrationally,

xìng hǎo dà bù fèn de xué sheng dōu méi yóu pǎo diào.
幸好大部份的學生都沒有跑掉 。
but, I kept most of my students.

(Cai finishes dressing. He is wearing his old People's Liberation Army uniform.)

CAI: Wǒ zhè shēn jiù jūn zhuāng! Hái tǐng hé shēn!
我這身舊軍裝！還挺合身 ！
My old army uniform! It still fits!

(Pause.)

Ní běn lái shì gè háo lǎo shī,
你本來是個好老師,
You're such a good teacher.

Hǎo hāo de zěn me qù zuò shēng yì ne?
好好的怎麼去做生意呢 ？
Why did you try to become a businessman?

PETER: Nǐ tīng shuō guò mǎ dé sēn wēn sī dùn bó shì ma?
你聽說過馬德森溫斯頓博士嗎？
Have you heard of Dr. Winston Madsen?

CAI: Dāng rán tīng guò! Tā shì yán jiū hàn shū de shì jiè quán wēi.
當然聽過！他是研究漢書的世界權威。
Of course! The world's authority on Han Dynasty calligraphy.

PETER: Fēi cháng chū sè de yí gè rén,
非常出色的一個人，
A brilliant man.

Wó yǐ qián shì tā de xué sheng.
我以前是他的學生。
I used to be his student.

CAI: Shì ma? Tā nián jì yīng gāi bù xiǎo le.
是嗎？他年紀應該不小了。
Really? He must be quite old now.

PETER: Qī shí sān.
七十三。
Seventy-three.

Hái zhù zài běi jīng.
還住在北京。
Still living in Beijing.

Qù nián wǒ qù kàn guò mǎ dé sēn bó shì,
去年我去看過馬德森博士，
I visited Dr. Madsen last year.

Tā yí gè rén zhù zài nà xiǎo gōng yù lǐ miàn,
他一個人住在那小公寓裡面，
He lives alone in his tiny flat,

děng zhe shén me rén gěi tā yí fèn gōng zuò,
等著什麼人給他一份工作，
waiting for anyone to offer him a job,

nà mèn zhe zì jǐ de rén shēng shì fǒu bái guò.
納悶著自己的人生是否白過 。
and wondering if he's wasted his life.

(Pause.)

Jú zhǎng,
局長，
Minister,

Wǒ bú yào biàn chéng zhè ge yàng zi.
我不要變成這個樣子 。
I didn't want to become like him.

CAI: Nǐ zhī dào ma,
你知道嗎，
You know,

wàn lǐ cháng chéng shì zhōng guó rén de jiāo ào.
萬里長城是中國人的驕傲 。
Chinese are quite proud of the Great Wall.

Suī rán méi yǒu dá dào fáng yù wài dí de shǐ mìng,
雖然沒有達到防禦外敵的使命，
Despite the fact that it was built to keep out foreigners,

yě jiù shì dāng chū jiàn zào tā de yuán yīn.
也就是當初建造它的原因 。
and utterly failed to do so.

Dàn shì wèi le jiàn zào lǐ miàn de yī zhuān yī shí,
但是為了建造裡面的一磚一石，
But in the bricks of that structure

xī shēng le bù zhī duō shǎo rén de xìng mìng,
犧牲了不知多少人的性命,
are many who died working on it,

tā men de gú tóu cháng mái dì xià, chéng wéi cháng chéng de
yí bù fen.
他們的骨頭長埋地下, 成為長城的一部份。
whose bones were ground down for building materials.

(Pause.)

Kě néng zhè yě shì wǒ gēn nǐ de mìng yùn, bú shì ma?
可能這也是我跟你的命運, 不是嗎?
Maybe that's like you and me, huh?

Wǒ men zhù dìng zàng shēn zài zhè dà jiàn zhù.
我們註定葬身在這大建築。
Born to be building materials.

Yí dàn xiǎng dào zhè diǎn, jiù ràng wǒ jué dé nǐ zhōng yú,
一旦想到這點, 就讓我覺得你終於,
Which makes you, I suppose, if I think about it,

yóu diǎn xiàng zhōng guó rén le.
有點像中國人了。
just a little bit Chinese.

(Cai begins singing the aria from "Presenting Pearl on the Hongqiao Bridge":)

Guāng huá yǒng yào . . .
光華永耀……
This pearl shines . . .

(His singing is interrupted by a loud banginig on a door, off-stage. Then the sound of police sirens.)

Wó dé zǒu le.

我得走了。

I'd better go.

(Cai starts to exit, Peter follows.)

Bù. Bié ràng rén jiā kàn jiàn nǐ gēn wǒ zài yī qǐ,

不。別讓人家看見你跟我在一起,

No. You can't be seen with me,

yào bù nǐ quán bù xué sheng dōu huì pǎo diào de,

要不你全部學生都會跑掉的,

or you will lose all your students.

Tā men bá wǒ dài zóu yǐ hòu nǐ cái lí kāi ba.

他們把我帶走以後你才離開吧。

Wait here until after they take me away.

(Rather than leaving, Peter, instead, resumes the song:)

PETER:

. . . Qíng bù yí.

……情不移。

. . . Forever like our love.

(Ignoring Cai's warning, Peter exits with him.
Crossfade to a meeting of the Guiyang Provincial Party Com-
mittee. Geming stands at a podium, addressing the gathering:)

GEMING: Běn rén yǒu xìng jiē rèn wéi guì yáng shì shì zhǎng!

本人有幸接任為貴陽市市長!

I humbly accept your appointment as Mayor of Guiyang!

Gǎn xiè nǐ men de xìn rèn!

感謝你們的信任!

Thank you for your trust!

Zhòng suǒ zhōu zhī, wǒ men de chéng shì jiāng yào miàn lín jù
dà de gǎi biàn le.
眾所周知，我們的城市將要面臨巨大的改變了。
As you know, great changes are coming to our city.

Zhuán yǎn jiān, xīn de wén huà zhōng xīn kuài yào wán chéng,
轉眼間，新的文化中心快要完成，
Already, the new Cultural Center is nearing completion.

yù jì jīn nián wǔ yuè kāi mù. Jiè shí shuài xiān dēng chǎng wéi
dà jiā biáo yǎn de shì
預計今年五月開幕。屆時率先登場為大家表演的是
It will open this May with a performance

fēi shēng guó jì de zhōng guó zá jì tuán!
蜚聲國際的中國雜技團！
by the world-famous Chinese Acrobats!

Guì yáng yào jǔ bù mài xiàng xīn shì jì le!
貴陽要舉步邁向新世紀了！
Guiyang is ready to step into the future!

(Cheers rise. Geming motions to Xi, offstage. She enters.)

Wǒ tài tai, xí yán, wén huà jú fù jú zhǎng.
我太太，席言，文化局副局長。
My wife, Xi Yan, Vice Minister of Culture.

XI: Wèi le chéng shì de jìn bù,
　　為了城市的進步，
　　We have all made sacrifices

wǒ men dōu zuò chū le xī shēng.
我們都作出了犧牲。
to bring progress to our city.

Xiàn zài, guì yáng zhōng yú gǎn shàng xīn zhōng guó de jiǎo bù le!

现在, 貴陽終於趕上新中國的腳步了！

Now, Guiyang is ready to join the New China!

(Flashbulbs pop. Geming and Xi wave to the gathering, looking every inch the perfect couple.)

Scene 13

(The American assembly room. Daniel is continuing his talk from the top of the play.)

DANIEL: So then that Judge took me to dinner, and gave me my first contract—for the Cultural Center. Soon after, he went on to become Mayor. Frankly, I lucked out. He recommended me for jobs in other provinces. And today, Ohio Signage and Outdoor Advertising operates in six Chinese cities, and we have just received our first order for work in Shanghai.

(Pause.)

I travel to China a lot now. Sometimes, with my wife and kids, who've gotten to love the place. When I'm over there, the Mayor and I always have dinner. We've become friends. That is a relationship I can never afford to jeopardize. My "Guanxi."

(Pause.)

To anyone considering working over there, I think it's important to enter the Chinese market with realistic expectations. I mean, there may have been a time when they looked up to us. If so, that was long before I came onto the scene. Nowadays, to be successful, you have to understand your place in their picture. Just be aware that you may not—well, I can almost assure you that you *will* not—get everything you want.

(Pause.)

And that may just have to be enough.

(Rows and rows of projected Chinese characters blanket the stage.)

There are over ten thousand Chinese characters. At Ohio Signage, it's our job to make sure our translations are correct. Maybe one day, all the signs will be fixed. But the funny thing is, I've sorta come to love the mistakes. There, in black and white, you can see that we really don't understand each other too well. So, for the foreseeable future, we'll all have to keep struggling—with Chinglish.

(The lights fade to black.)

END OF PLAY

DAVID HENRY HWANG's plays include *M. Butterfly* (1988 Tony Award; 1989 Pulitzer Prize finalist), *Golden Child* (1996 Obie Award; 1998 Tony nomination), *Yellow Face* (2008 Obie Award; 2008 Pulitzer Prize finalist) and *FOB* (1981 Obie Award). His Broadway musicals include the books for *Elton John & Tim Rice's Aida* (co-author), *Flower Drum Song* (2002 revival; 2003 Tony nomination) and Disney's *Tarzan*. According to *Opera News*, he is America's most produced living opera librettist, who has written four works with composer Philip Glass, as well as Osvaldo Golijov's *Ainadamar* (two 2007 Grammy Awards), Unsuk Chin's *Alice in Wonderland* and Bright Sheng's *The Silver River*. He penned the feature films *M. Butterfly*, *Golden Gate* and *Possession* (co-writer), and co-wrote the song "Solo" with pop star Prince. From 1994–2000, he served by appointment of President Clinton on the President's Committee on the Arts and the Humanities. He currently sits on the boards of The Dramatists Guild of America, American Theatre Wing and Lark Play Development Center. Hwang attended Stanford University and the Yale School of Drama. He is the recipient of the 2011 PEN/Laura Pels International Foundation for Theater Award for a Master American Dramatist.